# CHASING HORNBILLS

## UP TO MY NECK IN AFRICA

SIMON FENTON

Published in 2016
by Eye Books
29A Barrow Street
Much Wenlock
Shropshire
TF13 6EN
www.eye-books.com

ISBN: 978-1-78563-026-2

British Library Cataloguing in Publication Data
A catalogue record for this book is available from the British Library

Printed by CPI Group (UK) Ltd, Croydon CR0 4YY

To my family and friends in Abéné

# CONTENTS

# FOREWORD

"So what do you do, then?" This is what I would ask people at parties and such like. My detractors would take issue with this, saying that I was superficial and that it was more rewarding to know what people are than what they do. Superficial, well, maybe I am, but I do like to know what people do; it goes some way towards defining them. Without this particular piece of context, people tend to appear in a vacuum of cold spiritual inclinations, and revolting predilections and habits.

Understandably many of us are reluctant to spill the beans on what we actually do, given that what most of us do – with our working lives at least – is utterly fatuous and devoid of meaning. We have been fooled, by Capitalism and the corporations and the besuited thugs who run the media, into trading those basic human rights of creativity, discovery, freedom, adventure and joy, for comfort and security, for ease and vanity. A crap deal if ever there was one, but it's true: from my investigations I have established that the great majority of people have never swum in a lake or a river, have never slept beneath the stars nor walked in the moonlight, nor even climbed some wild and distant hill. Poor misguided wretches; soon they will find themselves on their death-beds, totting up the reckoning.

"Did I drink to the full the joys and glories that were set before me upon the table of life?"

All too often the answer will be "No, I didn't want to run the risk, or lose my job in the design and marketing of baubles to fool the foolish into parting with more of their money; I didn't fancy getting wet and cold or a little bit scared...so I stayed in and watched the telly."

When it all boils down to it you've only got yourself to blame, but it may not be too late to do something about it. You've got the book in your hand, now read it, and then act upon it. We can't all be Semen Fenton (Senegalese pronunciation), but we can take a leaf from his book and get out there and walk a little on the wild side. Because Simon Fenton certainly has taken life by the balls, and better still, he has the gift of being able to communicate it. It's still a long way off; he's young, but I assure you that when his time is up, Simon will be able to slip away in peace, because he has lived a real life and rejoiced in the fabulous and varied wonders of the world. And it's a comforting thought, to be able to die easy.

There's a whole genre of this sort of book, and they are written by people who are blessed by curiosity and daring and a healthy disdain for the conventional way...and cursed perhaps, by *Vermittlungsdrang* (sometimes only a

German word will do, and in this case it means "urge to communicate"). Fenton does the *Vermittlung* well; his style is easy and his experiences irresistibly fascinating...and you like him...and you like even more Khady, his wonderful Senegalese wife, who is the kingpin of the whole shebang.

The genre – self-help, travel, lifestyle – it's all of these and yet none of these, but good, anyway – is there for inspiration. It worked for me: I was inspired back in my time by Laurie Lee, Gerald Brenan, Paddy Leigh-Fermor, and having read them and others, made decisions in my life according to what I had learned from their books, and it stood me in good stead.

So go on, read the book, and then act upon it. You could start by checking out the Little Baobab, Khady and Simon's guest house in the Casamance. I would certainly do it myself, except that I would have to miss my favourite television programme.

*Chris Stewart*
El Valero, August 2016

# SENEGAL AND THE CASAMANCE

DAKAR

BANJUL

TH

◆ BRIKAMA
◆ MADINA DAFFE
ABÉNÉ ◆
◆ KAFOUNTINE
HAERE ◆ ◆ BIGNONA
◆ ZIGUINCHOR
DJEMBERING ◆

100KM

BISSAU

BUBAQUE ◆

BIJAGOS ISLANDS

MAURITANIA

ENEGAL

MALI

AMBIA

ASAMANCE

GUINEA
BISSAU

◆ TAMBACOUNDA

NIOKOLOKOBA
NATIONAL PARK

BASSARI LANDS

◆ ETHIOLO

GUINEA

As with my first book, although one or two names have been changed and minor modifications of chronology made, everything in this book did happen. However, interpretations, and indeed misinterpretations, are my own. For explanations of unfamiliar words not explained within the text, please refer to the glossary at the back of the book.

Oh, and anyone of a delicate disposition might prefer to skip the fourth chapter.

# THE HEART OF LIGHTNESS

*I'm driving down the smugglers' route with Omar. We pass through the forest, down from the Gambia to Abéné, across the border in Senegal. After weeks in England it's exhilarating to speed through mile after mile of vivid green forest and lakes of mud through which Kermit, my fluorescent green Land Rover, slithers and slides. As we cross an open patch of land, I spot two large birds pecking at the ground.*

*They're huge – perhaps a metre tall each. Omar screeches to a halt, leaps out and runs towards them, flapping his arms and squawking like a bird himself. The two birds, Abyssinian ground hornbills, start running, then take off, and I see a flash of white beneath their black wings as they only just clear the trees. Bemusedly, for I thought I'd heard it all by now, I ask a slightly breathless Omar what's going on.*

*"Simon, this bird is very special to the Diola people and we always make it fly if we see one; otherwise we will have bad luck."*

*Not long after, I was sitting on the roadside while my Land Rover was being fixed. It was nearly finished when I felt a large splat on my leg. Africans aren't the only ones with bird-related superstitions…*

*Back in Abéné, I go to see my African mother, Diatou. She will often explain the finer points of Diola culture to me and I want to check if hornbills held any deeper meanings for the Diola; they don't – or if they do, she isn't telling.*

*"But Simon, don't you remember when we went to Ziguinchor with Tom?"*

*Of course I remembered that trip. Khady and I had taken a car with Diatou and her late husband Tom, who had died while we were there. Then Khady and I had taken a bus back, and it had crashed en route, nearly killing us both.*

*"Well, we saw that bird on the way there and I told the driver to stop, but he just carried on."*

*We'd neglected to chase hornbills that day, and seemingly paid the price.*

*Over the coming months, when I experience tropical illness, near death, voodoo madness and seriously question my own sanity, I find myself wondering if I should have joined Omar and chased them today.*

I arrive back in Abéné with fresh eyes, following a two-month absence. I feel a renewed sense of wonder and recognition of the place as my true paradise after the harshness of the Sahara, the bleakness of the Sahel, the freezing cold of Europe and the workaholism of England. Once again I've travelled overland from Europe to Senegal, but unlike the funk I'd been in the first time, I am joyful about returning to Africa, to Khady and my children. Even the Mauritanian iron-ore train, a two-mile-long goods wagon where I froze and was sandblasted while being chucked around for hours on end, couldn't wipe the grin off my face.

I have never felt surer that this is where I want to be. My family is safe and healthy and happy, and so am I. To think how different my life could have turned out if I had not crossed the Sahara five years ago, so unaware of what lay ahead... Now I feel clear. I have jumped and a net has appeared. I have met someone special. I have started a family. I have bought some land and started to build and run the Little Baobab, an eco guest house and tour business. I have friends, and I feel part of something meaningful at last.

Gulliver is waiting by the gate as I arrive home. He is barefoot in a pair of shorts, and eating rice from an old plastic bowl. When he sees me he puts the bowl on his head, but for the next few days he won't let go of me, clinging on day and night. Although speaking mainly Diola, he remembers his English, now referring to himself in the third person as "the monkey boy".

After a joyful reunion with Khady and the extended family, I set off again; I want to re-acquaint myself immediately with the village and its people. This is still a dry spring heat, bearable despite the temperature. In fact, pleasant, for me, as my body has not yet forgotten the chill of England.

I follow narrow sandy lanes where the cows and goats

roam free. When Gulliver walks here with me he shouts the names of all the trees with the same excitement as if he's been given sweets: "Mango! Cashew! Palm!"

The children next door are excited to see me and cry out "*toubab*," "Simon," or "Daddy," a term I've become known as locally. They run out to follow me, a blur of bare feet, dusty skin and snotty faces, shrieking, then beating a hasty retreat when I stop or move to approach them. Who needs the *kankurang* when I'm around?

I pass the local shop, where Barrie, a tall thin man, invariably in a *boubou*, greets me. Today he's with a friend and they call out some extra words in Fula, their language. I don't understand a single word and, for all I know, he's shouting "salad" at me. Probably not though, as all conversations follow pretty much the same pattern:

"*Assalaamu alaykum* or *bonjour* or hello or *kassumei* or nagadef*"

"How are you?"

"*Kokobo* (Fine)."

"How's your family?"

"*Kokobo*."

"How's your house?"

"*Kokobo*."

"How are you?"(Again.)

"*Kokobo*." (Still.)

"How's Khady?"

"*Kokobo*."

"How are you?"

"*Kokobo.*"

"Where's Khady?"

"*Om bo sindeye* (at home)."

"How are the little ones?"

"*Kokobo.*"

"Where are they?"

"*Om bo sindeye.*"

"How are you?"

"*Kokobo.*" (Still.)

"Where are you going?"

"Village."

"*Kermit oh mey*?" (No one can understand why I'd walk when I have a vehicle).

"*Om bo sindey – Leggy leggy* (I go right now)."

"*Ça va?*"

By this point I've gone.

Sometimes this seems to go on forever, with plenty of '*ça va*'s thrown in during conversational lulls. I've noticed that often people will declare your name out of the blue, joyfully. I'll be sitting, staring into the middle distance, surrounded by people, and someone will heartily declare "Simon!" I think this shows that they remember your name, but perhaps more importantly, it's an acknowledgement that you are there; a sign of respect.

Opposite the shop is a tiny mosque, just a simple *banku* room with water jugs outside, a zinc corrugated roof and a loudspeaker. The only time I hear the sunrise call to prayer is when we have guests, during which times it always seems to boom louder – at earsplitting volumes. There was a phase when they broadcast religious lectures on the radio over the distorted loudspeaker, usually between about 6am and 7am. I fantasised about visiting in the middle of the night to cut the wires, but in the end I realised that I'm the one who has to fit in.

Ironically, the house next door to the mosque is of the Balanta tribe – Christians from Guinea Bissau – and is it is a *dagga*, a drinking den. Occasionally I'll stop by to drink *cadeau*, fermented cashew fruit juice, from empty mayonnaise jars. At about 10p for two litres, it's affordable, and although it tastes like regurgitated pineapple juice, I rather like it. Swedish visitors, clearly of the glass-half-full disposition, declared it to taste like sherry, which will probably make for a better marketing campaign. This time I cry "*aye lama lama*" (cheers) to the motley collection of drunk rasta boys and continue on my way.

Beyond this house is a small dwelling belonging to the chief of our sector, which is named "Tranquil." Aside from the mosque, it is. He's a serious-looking old man, always in a *boubou* and skull cap, often teaching the Quran to a gaggle of kids clutching their wooden prayer boards. He also digs wells.

There's a track leading down to the village centre through a forest of cashew trees. It's cool and pretty. I pass Bert's house. He bought land recently and has built a roundhouse of mud, decorated artistically with shells and bits of kembo wood. Bert is the Dutch artist and a former Mickey Mouse at Disneyland, who paints the covers of my books. You meet all sorts in Abéné. He's not there, so I carry on, passing a few *banku* huts and a field of cows, and finally reaching the main street by a shack where Bouba repairs motorcycles, and a Mauritanian, called – like seemingly every Mauritanian man I know – Mohammed, runs a general store, which sells all the same stuff as all the other mostly Mauritanian stores staffed by Mohammeds.

Sacks of rice, sugar and onions, plastic containers of oil, sachets of tomato purée, bread spread (the local margarine that lasts forever without refrigeration and tastes furry; I prefer to go without), mayonnaise, sticks of *tapalapa* and so on. Tapa-lapa-tapa-lapa goes the sound as they pound the dough of these French-style baguettes. Outside, a couple of women stir peanuts, which grow like weeds here, in a sand-filled cauldron over a fire, while another spreads out old secondhand clothes to sell. This is where your charity bag donations end up.

Opposite is a bar decorated with gaudy crocodiles and palm trees sculpted from cement. Our gardener Fakeba's friend "Family" made this and has threatened to make us concrete crocodiles and other animals for our garden.

I walk past, towards Lipali's *quincaillerie*, where some of our building materials were bought. Outside, Lipali, a tall friendly man, chats with Omar the driver and Fitty Futta over cups of *attaya*, the strong sweet local tea. Fitty Futta (try saying that after a few beers) is a friend of Khady's, and often does odd jobs for us, although he does have a tendency to shout about everything and just be ever so slightly annoying for no discernible reason.

We exchange greetings and I tell them about my newspaper articles advertising Abéné. They're very happy, and flick through my first book, smiling at the pictures and pointing out those they know. Lipali tells me his shop is my home and I am welcome any time to eat, drink or "blah blah".

Everyone is greeting me: "Simon. Où est Khady?" and so on. I always find myself humming The Who's "Who are you? Who, who...who, who..." It's so easy for them; they can easily remember the names of the handful of *toubabs* living here. About 3,000 people know my name but I can't possibly remember all of theirs. Well, it could be 2,000, or perhaps 4,000, who know my name. I could just go out and count, then insert the correct number, but that's a bit too much effort.

The sense of community is strong, and although it's easy to be cynical and wonder about people's motivations, it feels natural enough. On a recent visit to a local nightclub, before I'd reached the bar I'd high-fived and fist-bumped half the guys in the village. I love living in a place where everyone knows each other's name.

At a row of ladies stirring, frying and serving from pots on fires at the roadside I speak to Fanta, then Farmatta and then yet another Binta. If I forget the name, I can usually say Binta, Khady, Mariama or Fatou, by which time I've covered 90% of Senegalese women. It's the same for men. If I walk into a busy place and shout Lamin or Moussa, half the blokes will turn round.

Then I hear a cry: "Hey, Big Man!"

"Petit Homme!" I call back to Cherif, Khady's cousin and one of the largest guys in town. He's a *djembe* drum teacher and runs the Makou bar. A lot of people call me big man. I may be six-foot tall, but I'm not that big. Although a year or two ago I may have been mildly offended, I've now discovered that the big man has power and commands respect. They're not referring specifically to size.

He enquires after my health, as I'd been sick last time we met: "How is de body?"

I enquire after Simon, his son, named after yours truly. All is good.

Meanwhile, we are surrounded by kids, all bearing baskets on their heads, selling things: "Peanuts?" "Cashews?" "Mandarin?" "*Fataya*?" and so on.

"Never buy food from people you don't know," Khady has warned me. "They might poison you, or cast a spell. Do you know women can add something to make you fall in love with them?" She has told me what, though she made me promise not to say, but it has put me off buying from strangers, and includes body parts that would stick in the teeth. I don't tend to eat out too often.

As a *toubab* in West Africa, you don't have to possess physical beauty or youth to attract the attention of someone who could probably have a career as a supermodel in the west. Even in remote Chinguetti, Mauritania, I've been approached.

A beautiful desert girl wearing a brightly patterned robe and headdress took me by the arm and, when no one was around, pulled me in close enough to feel her firm body, so close that I felt intoxicated by her musky perfume and could see tiny beads of sweat on her brow as she breathed sensually.

"Where's your wife?"

"In Senegal."

"No wife in Mauritania? Now you have one."

Well, I say, I hadn't expected that in the seventh holiest city of Islam.

Even now, several years after arrival, I was still regularly accosted by Binta, whom I affectionately think of as the "jiggy-jiggy woman." She still maintains that, as she saw me before I met Khady, she commands some kind of right over me, but that doesn't stop her chatting up every male *toubab* new in town. The other girls of Abéné, knowing and respecting Khady, tend to keep their distance, but further afield is a different story.

I pass the hospital where Gulliver was born and then see Papis' shack with its motley collection of trinkets, although I've never seen him actually sell anything. He greets me, handing over a USB stick. Papis is one of the few people here who likes Western music – and not just the obvious stuff; he's got very eclectic tastes, having spent time in Paris. "Have you got any Nirvana or Massive Attack?" he asks.

Next door is Dukou's new restaurant. She's Bert's wife, and runs this while he's busy building his house. There's an outdoor area fenced off with creotine, a kind of woven basket-like material used to make walls. There's no one there and when I enter, a monkey tethered to the bar stares back. I demand a drink but it doesn't understand, so on I go.

A young guy with dreads and dark glasses, large, scowling but looking very cool, approaches. I don't recognise him and avoid his stare. I can spot a "bumster" at 20 paces, but he veers towards me.

"How is de holiday?"

"What holiday?" That baffles him.

"I is Skippy innit," he says in a Gambian-London accent, pulling out cheap plastic rasta bracelets and trying to force one upon me. It's a common tactic to give something cheap that you probably don't want, in order to make you feel guilty and buy something else.

As a middle-class English white boy, I guess it's an instinctive response to feel threatened by African men. Whatever the reality, years of media propaganda of angry guys waving machetes, of black youth crime in London and so on have conditioned me, rightly or wrongly, to feel that. In all of my years in Asia, I never really felt threatened, even when I was shaken down at knife-point in a Shanghai night club. I was a foot taller than the average guy for a start. But, in Africa it's different: body language, the physical size of people, facial expressions, conversations that are often shouted and, predominantly, the aforementioned media-induced preconceptions. Of course, it's mostly nonsense, and the moment you smile, the big scary guy breaks into a heart-warming grin and turns out to be a big softie.

Although I never normally feel danger in Abéné, a tourist was recently robbed at knife-point by an outsider. Skippy is a big guy, and I feel slightly anxious, deciding skulduggery may be afoot, so quickly push on as he declares me a bad man for not wanting to talk.

Another dreadlocked rasta is approaching on his motorbike, this time a paler, *toubab* one. Miguel is a Portuguese dude who runs a permaculture project in nearby Kafountine. In fact, the Portuguese have long had an impact on African agriculture, having introduced maize and manioc in the 16th century.

Still in his late twenties, Miguel has spent the best part of a decade in Africa, running a bar just inside the Guinea Bissau border for several years and then starting up a number of permaculture gardens. We discuss a film I'd made of his recent performance. As well as DJ-ing and gardening, Miguel is a reggae drummer (of course) and recently performed at Abéné's second biggest night of the year.

The biggest is New Year's Eve, when several thousand people from across Senegal, along with tourists, congregate upon the beach for what have been some of the best parties of my life. The second biggest is the 11 May celebration, the anniversary of Bob Marley's death, when every bar, nightclub and sound system in Abéné kicks off. Miguel's band, the African Roots Rockers, performed, while a variety of guys got up and sang Bob's greatest hits to an ecstatic crowd. Although my film could never capture the intensity of the performance, I was pleased with the result and promised to give Miguel a copy.

I call in to see a pal. Soulyman is a dreadlocked *mamapara* (stilt dancer) who may win the prize for friendliest chap in Abéné. He is out and has chalked upon the wall of his house, "I've gone to a village to watch football. See you down the road." I pick a piece of charcoal from the fire and leave my message on the wall. A standard method of communication in these parts.

I see a broken-down quad bike by the side of the road. I know it belongs to my friend Deanne. I'm no longer the only Brit in the village year-round. Deanne, of Anglo-Ghanian heritage, radiates love, and seemingly lives either to help people or to fix her quad bike (a bit like me with Kermit). She's not there, but I'm prompted to visit her soon as we regularly exchange films, seeds and plants.

There's another local bar where I stop for a refreshment but they don't have any drinks, according to the large lethargic lady who has yet to attend a customer-service training workshop. On I go.

I'm glad I do, as I bump into one of my best friends. Crazy Jack is the bighearted Dutch man who has built a rather wonderful house in the jungle and an equally wonderful school for the local kids, balancing his time down here with truck-driving in Northern Europe to feed the coffers. He also has a rather amusing name that never fails to make me giggle.

"Simon, let me tell you, my name, Jack Wijnker, is pronounced Jaques Vanker but I wanted to Anglicise it when travelling, so I named myself Jack Wanker. I had no idea what this meant but I noticed the English were very happy people. They were always laughing when they met me. Simon, I am proud to be a Wanker. My Grandfather was a Wanker, my father was a Wanker, I am a Wanker and my children are little Wankers."

Moving on, I pass Wassolon's drum shop, Gerard's restaurant, Yula's hardware store, Serin Fall's car workshop (a greasy patch of earth and a few old wrecks under a mango tree), the Nelson Mandela English/French school, José the Spaniard's restaurant, another Lamin who mends shoes, Raoul the Fula with his small general store, the *djibiterie* where they grill lamb, and where I've often been tempted to try the 'cow foot and empty chips', Ortos who makes wooden furniture under a tree, countless lads selling art for tourists, often made from old mobile phones, oil cans and other junk, my friend Bass the tailor and more, more, many more. Each wants me to stop and run through the greeting outlined above, which is why I often cycle or take Kermit. And if I'm with Khady she'll chat for ages with each. It can take us an hour or two to walk the one kilometre to the beach.

An old man on a bicycle beckons me over. With a conspiratorial wink he opens a bag strapped to a rack over the back wheel. I glance in to see a flash of green and, heart racing with excitement, hand over my cash. It's not a common crop in these parts and for the first time in a year here, I have myself some courgettes.

Local tastes are very conservative and Khady won't touch them, so I'm now thinking about whether to chop them up with tomatoes and whip up a ratatouille-type concoction, or grill them slowly over the fire with a little salt, pepper and olive oil. Mmm, my mouth's watering at the thought. It's these simple pleasures that make me happy. Happier in fact than when I have everything easily available in supermarkets or to buy at the click of a button. The struggle to find things sure makes you appreciate them more.

Before reaching the beach, I take a left turn down a track past Cherif's Makou bar and on towards the *bolong*, a low area that turns into a swamp during the rainy season. Bert was once wading across this and thought he saw a crocodile, which turned out to be a log, so we all had a good laugh. There's usually plenty of birds to be seen and it's a pretty spot, only a couple of hundred metres from our place. I continue up, back into the shade of cashews and along the track to our house. As I approach, I hear the cries of "Daddy". Not only Gulliver, but Fakeba, our young Gambian gardener. They're together, putting mulch around the flowers. Everyone calls me Daddy, even Fakeba's father, who must be in his 60s.

The new cat, Marina, tangles around my feet, and little Gulliver runs towards me, tripping as he approaches, but so excited that he forgets to cry, and leaps into my arms. Khady, who is pulling water out of the well, declares I'm a "salty homme" and sends me to the shower. When I finish she is ladling a broth of vegetables and fish into a bowl. It's delicious; like an African version of French *bouillabaisse*.

I feel very at home on my land, and sometimes even find myself forgetting how life was back in England. The odd things become normalised until I am reminded by guests fresh from Europe that perhaps it's not typical for chickens to jump up on the table as we eat. Or that to transport a cow along with ourselves in a canoe is not a normal state of affairs. Or that a driver kicking you to indicate that the car is about to leave and you need to get in is an acceptable level of customer service. Or that tomato ketchup is a satisfactory base sauce for a pizza.

I sit down on my verandah and look out to the purple sunset and the silhouettes of my palm trees, gazing as intently as if I were watching television, while eating a homegrown guava the size of a large grapefruit, surrounded by my people and a deep tranquility.

As darkness falls, we do as man has done for millennia, and sit by the fire, alternating staring into the flames with looking up at the incredible starlit sky. Africans don't put their kids to bed early; everyone just lives to the rhythm of the day, as we're not bound to the nine-to-five lifestyle. Often there is a little drumming, when Khady and the kids will dance. Gulliver takes after me with his natural rhythms, whereas Alfie has a more unique dancing style, like his mother. (Or should that be the other way around?)

Life in Africa is, for me at least, sweet, and for the time being I've forgotten about those hornbills.

# TERANGA: FEELING AT HOME

Teranga *is a word you hear a lot in Senegal, a Wolof word, meaning hospitality or welcoming generosity. It's one of the many things that makes Senegal so special in my eyes, and is at the core of the culture.*

*When Khady cooks, she prepares a large bowl of rice with fish and sauce, which our staff, kids and various hangers-on crouch around to eat with their hands. If we happen to have a carpenter doing a job, a taxi driver has dropped someone off or somebody is wandering past – even a stranger – then they are beckoned over to join in. That's* teranga.

*When the choicest morsels are flicked in my direction on the plate, that's* teranga.

*When I rock up in a remote village and the Chief sends out for drinks and makes up beds without even asking if I need a place to stay, that's* teranga.

*Value isn't measured by how much you have, but by how much you give. That's* teranga.

*It's one reason I love living here, although I must admit that when Fitty Futta just happens to turn up exactly as we're serving dinner every night for weeks on*

> *end, my* toubab *side shines through, and I can't help*
> *wondering where* teranga *ends and urinal extraction*
> *begins. I suppose, as an Englishman, I feel making others*
> *welcome must ultimately have its limits – so that we can*
> *make ourselves fully at home, perhaps. It's been tough*
> *enough work making this home for ourselves...*

My garden is blooming, the sea is warm, the food fresh, the *teranga* overwhelming and, as always in Abéné, the drums beat night and day. I have arrived back just in time for Gulliver's third birthday, so we bake a lemon cake in our mud oven. It is a beautiful day.

Neighbours with drums show up and start dancing, then stay on through the evening. Gulliver wows us all on the dance floor, before running scared from the *mamapara*, a masked stilt dancer who unsuccessfully tries to whisk him up for a bird's eye view of our land.

Gulliver is no longer the only little baobab in town though. Alphaseyne Harry Fenton, or Alfie, joined us during the previous rainy season. On a particularly hot and oppressively humid day, Khady declared during breakfast that she thought we'd better go to the hospital. I got up with a start, only to be told to sit down and finish my coffee.

Later on there was a huge crack of thunder, a massive downpour of rain, the lights went out, and out popped Alfie. At more than 4kg, he was big, so everyone had been telling us there would be twins. They did the same with my first son, Gulliver. As Khady lay exhausted, I was left peering at her deflated belly wondering where the other baby was.

My job was to fan her as her aunt brought food and water and fussed around as, typically for an African hospital, it is the family's responsibility to organise food, bedding and so on. The nurses were competent, although not exactly blessed with a bedside manner, and the power cut was also typical. But there was a back-up battery and it was no big deal. This is Africa.

Alfie is growing fast, and started walking at seven months. He has a beautiful smile and a happy nature, and beeps and buzzes like a little unstoppable, indestructible robot, always busy and constantly both delighting and exhausting us. When Soulyman the *mamapara* gives up trying to lift Gulliver, Alfie has no such qualms about being scooped up, and is not in the least bit fazed.

I really enjoy spending time with Gulliver now that he is talking, running around and forming a headstrong little character. The monkey boy is a happy boy and, by the time he was three, he was already speaking English, French, Diola, Mandinka and Wolof. I take him and Alfie to the beach several times a week and Gulliver is becoming more confident in the waves, having swum with me since he was six weeks old. One day we saw an older French lady enter the ocean.

"Look Daddy – *toubab*!" said Gulliver.

"What am I?"

"You're a daddy-bab."

"And what are you?"

"I'm the Gulliver," he said, diving back into the waves, laughing.

There are many comedy moments. One day he ran towards me crying "*Foo koff! Foo koff!*" I was about to get angry with someone for teaching him that when Khady saw my surprise and said, "But don't you know? *Foo koff* is Diola for 'head'." It turned out he'd scratched his head and it was *buco-buco* (painful).

The kids are free-range, climbing trees, playing in the sand and worrying our guests when they sit too close to the fire. They've grown up with fire and animals. There are plenty of eyes watching them and yes, occasionally they get a minor burn, but that's how they learn.

Along with the children, there are also the animals. Life for pets in Africa tends to the tough. Our first four dogs, Toubab, Scrappy, Mango and Bandit, were all either stolen or succumbed to snakes or unknown illnesses, but Ketchup has been going strong for more than a year. Incidentally, the name is my spelling of his traditional Diola name, which sounds something like "Cachup". He's a friendly chap, and I often drag him around the village on a leash, which he strains at to give chase to monkeys and lizards. We were also given a kitten, which Gulliver named Marina, after one of our English friends. She in turn went on to have kittens and we kept one, Bruce the Moose. Moose is the Wolof word for cat. And "cat" is the Diola word for "stop."

"Gulliver, cat!"

It's all very confusing.

The cats eat only leftovers but they are in good condition and we haven't seen a mouse since their arrival. In addition, we still have chickens, albeit an uncountable number. Khady usually knows how many and occasionally we will eat fresh eggs for breakfast. Only occasionally though, as the feed quality is low in protein.

"We need to feed them eggs if we want them to give us eggs," says Fakeba, our young Gambian gardener. That, to me, seems to defeat the object.

I'm soon settled back into a routine, getting up in the morning to water and tend the garden with Fakeba before the heat builds up, or I'm attacked by mosquitos or tsetse flies or baffe, the prickly bush that is everywhere and can cause a dull ache for days if it stabs you, which it regularly does. Luckily we don't get too many dangerous creatures like snakes on our land...

...Well, there were a couple of puff adders we found while clearing the bush. Unlike most serpents, they stay put when they hear you coming – and will bite – but you have a day or so to get the antidote, so no worries. Then there was the two-metre-long skin shed by a python that I found not long after moving here. I also mustn't forget the green mamba in the kitchen. Oh, and the black cobra in the toilet. Then there was the unidentified blue and red striped snake...but apart from these, we don't really get too many snakes...

Little by little we have been developing our house, our land and our lives. I say little by little, but actually we have achieved a remarkable amount in just a few years in which, between us, we've built five houses, raised two children, developed a travel business, travelled around, written and published two books, and much more. The secret of such productivity? I don't have an internet connection at home.

We've made a *château* – a water tower into which we pump water from the well. This then feeds into the tap, shower and toilets. Running water may be a human right in the West, but here in Senegal it's still not a given. After several years of bucket showers, turning that tap on for the first time was a 'wow' moment.

We try to reduce our living costs by living as self-sufficiently as possible: I don't have any utility bills; the fruit trees are coming along nicely; we have some modest vegetable success and, as the garden develops, I hope to produce more and more of our own food.

Our garden and forest areas have been coming on very well over the past couple of years, although it's always one step forwards and two steps back. Fakeba and I work hard for months and everything is flourishing, then heavy rains or a break-in goat destroy our crops. It's harsh, and there's little respite from the sun that kills some plants, the desert-like dry-season aridity or the trench-like mud-bath of the rains. We provide *teranga* to the monkeys, squirrels, wild cats and other creatures who pop in for their fill of ripe fruit and vegetables. It can be heartbreaking to find your entire aubergine crop eaten after months of careful watering.

My philosophy has been to try to keep everything as natural as possible, and to combine the practical with aesthetics, so I mix fruit trees, vegetables and medicinal plants alongside pretty flowers and plants. I don't like straight lines in the garden and wanted to avoid its looking like an orchard, preferring to develop what I call a "forest garden".

I have been battling with Fakeba, who has a tendency to follow the traditional agricultural methods, ploughing the same sections every year, then planting maize and beans – to little effect, as the soil nutrients are long since depleted. He works hard but is none too eager to heed my advice.

"Fakeba, you did this last year and we didn't have any corn growing."

"But it may grow this year; God is great," he replies, without the evidence to back this up.

The only solution is to try my own methods, and to persist. Surely he can't deny actual visual evidence? The experiment is under way...

I'm all for trying to keep things simple, natural and rustic but I've had a hard time explaining that to Fakeba. I've elucidated my philosophy a dozen times, only for him to decide to paint a tree white or, on one occasion, make a concrete heart-shaped border around a flower-bed, which the locals loved, but I thought tacky. So, when I was away for a while and called home to hear Khady tell of a surprise she'd made for me in the garden, a chill ran through my heart as I remembered the concrete crocodile Fakeba had told me he wanted to construct.

I needn't have worried. Khady clearly understands my taste, and had made a lovely breakfast area: a mosaic-tiled floor, so as to protect the bamboo furniture, which would swiftly be destroyed by termites if left on bare earth, and three wooden umbrellas with thatched parasols.

This process of making ourselves at home and comfortable has at times been complicated by cross-cultural confusions. Some interesting issues have arisen from instances where one culture "just knows" things the other...just doesn't.

One day a European friend living nearby showed me a coat hanger that a worker had broken and then attempted to mend by gluing the hook on to the end of the hanger, as opposed to in the middle where it belonged. Of course, why would he know? No one uses coat hangers here, but it sure made us giggle.

My friend Fitty Futta, when not eating my food, is a tiler. I hired him to decorate our bathroom, and he did a great job, apart from one detail. He made a shallow basin, like a shower tray, around the plughole. All well and good – except that it was more than a metre away from the wall where the shower head was attached.

We may laugh at such things, but it works both ways. Imagine how many simple things taken for granted by Africans we must get wrong. Khady thought me a complete and utter imbecile when I revealed that I was fairly inept at coping when toilet paper wasn't available – which is always, unless I carry it. Africans, like the people of most developing nations, use water and their left hand. As a result, using your left hand for eating is very bad form. They find the notion of using paper about as disgusting as we find the idea of using your hand. This is kids' stuff in Africa. And how come it often takes me more than two or three matches to light a fire? Am I totally incompetent? No need to answer.

At times, although the local has the know-how, he doesn't feel it is appropriate to share his professional expertise – until it is too late. Our well was a case in point. The water, although potable, was coming out with a little muddy sediment. We called the well digger, Mustafa, and asked why we had this problem.

"It's because it's been dug in the wrong place. It's too close to trees, and their roots have penetrated the well wall, making the water muddy."

"So why did you build it there?"

"Because you told me to."

Thus I learnt yet another lesson about working in Africa.

On their first visit, my parents expressed concern about the well. "With young children, you should put a lid on it," they wisely counselled.

"But everyone has a well here," I declared. "Children don't need mollycoddling; they'll learn."

"Yes, but next door's boy fell in the well," Khady piped up.

The next day found me at the carpenter's, organising wood for the cover.

My lack of local know-how also got me into trouble when I decided to improve my home by putting up some shelves.

There is a common assumption here that *toubabs* can't do manual work, so when I told Fitty Futta I needed some bookshelves, he told me this was a specialist job, quoting a fee of several hundred pounds to stick a few planks of wood on the wall. I decided to prove this *toubab* is perfectly capable of manual work.

But I couldn't just pop to Ikea.

First I had to find someone who was chopping up a tree and get him to cut me some shelf-shaped pieces. Then I had to transport these to the guy who has a planing and sandpapering machine. Then I had to make my own brackets from other bits of wood. Then I found the wood was not fully dry, and it warped and shrank, and I had to turn it over every few weeks to bend it the other way. Then I discovered the wood was full of termites – and the whole thing disintegrated.

So I had to start again.

I took the new pieces of shelf wood to the sandman and stood watching as sawdust flew everywhere. Minutes later, my eyes started stinging. Rather than gradually ease off, the stinging intensified until I was writhing on the ground, dry-retching in agony. I went to lie in the back of Kermit, shaking as if having a seizure. Ibou, the sandman, then told me the type of wood I was using had a resin that could burn the eyes of some people. Clearly I was one of them.

By the time Khady led me to the beach, I was blind, and I staggered along as she clutched my arm. I dunked my head in the sea and a couple of young rasta guys brought a bowl of fresh water for me to rinse my eyes – all to no avail. Tears were streaming, the flesh red raw and the pain not even close to easing, and by now I was vomiting as well.

Unable to drive, Khady called a driver to take us home, where I fell into a deep sleep. Waking several hours later, I found the skin around my eyes was sore but I could see again, and by the next day I was feeling hunky dory. Perhaps I should have hired Monsieur Futta.

Still, eventually these things get fixed, and my house is becoming slowly more and more like a home.

African families are elastic in nature. The concept of four or five people locking themselves in a house and not knowing their neighbours is unheard of, and it's not unusual to enter a family compound with several houses for the co-wives, aunties, uncles and tens of kids. Enter at meal times and you'll be fed, even if you've eaten already.

Aside from the immediate family, we live with Fakeba, Yama, a very tall, slender and strikingly pretty Gambian girl who cooks and cleans, Jumbo, the girl we'd unofficially adopted, and also, by now, Khady's niece Myamoona, who is five years old. She is the daughter of Tierno, the *marabout* who had predicted Gulliver's birth, and who had now distinguished himself by leaving Khady's sister and their four small children for another woman, so we were relieving the pressure by taking in Myamoona for a while.

And let's not forget of course our rotating cast of hangers-on, such as Fitty Futta. And there's always someone new around; today, Khady's cousin Insa has dropped by. Khady has little patience with idlers, and although there's always room at the rice bowl, no one gets to relax too much. She immediately puts visitors to work. She's the grand matriarch, directing operations from the centre, making sure the kids are looked after, that I'm healthy and comfortable, that each of her businesses is running properly, that the guest rooms are prepared, food is cooking for the ten or more people, that the correct plants and vegetables are planted at the right time, and that fish has been bought for her sister to sell at her village in the dusty interior. When all of that is done Khady will dance.

I like Insa, who has been put to work watering the garden with Fakeba. It has come on a long way since his last visit.

"Oh Simon, Africa might be hell for the black man but it's paradise for the white man," he tells me. He doesn't say it, but he is probably also thinking that the West is paradise for the black man.

I can see what he means; it's true that job prospects are bleak here, but I do think he's undervaluing the quality of life. I think about some of the things I enjoy, the reasons why I love my life here: fresh food every day, the tranquil rural atmosphere, the free and safe environment for kids, the sense of family and community, endless sunshine, different fruits in season each month, the adventure and the otherworldliness of everyday things.

The cost of one cappuccino in England would feed an entire African family for a day or two. And, besides the high prices, the seriously cold fresh air and the seriously busy people, among the first things I notice on return to the UK is the amazing army of signs, notices, barriers, cameras and so on controlling the population. Hardly seems like paradise to me.

Actually, even here in Senegal, such controlling mechanisms put in the odd, intrusive appearance. On one occasion, "sleeping policemen" appeared in one day when a main road was resurfaced. They weren't there when I was driving to Ziguinchor in the morning, but I nearly shook my teeth out hitting them at 60 mph on my return. One young motorcyclist was less fortunate, losing his life to them, as they were virtually invisible at night.

I travel around Senegal and West Africa a fair bit, and it's true that the inland villages certainly can be pretty bleak and dusty. Geography and harsh climates play a large role in Africa's failure to reach its potential, and were I from these dusty parts, I'm sure I'd be keen to escape via what is known locally as "the back way" to Europe, across the Sahara Desert and Libya. But many of the emigrants I hear about actually originally hail from places that I have described as idyllic, tranquil and so on.

The grass is always greener, I suppose, though one set of problems tends to replace another. Of course, I'm a Westerner – not particularly well-off by European standards, but I grew up with running water, electricity, television and pretty much everything I needed. I am now in a position to choose to go back to nature, to a simpler life. But I can see this simple life could seem like hell for a local person who has no fall-back if the crops don't grow, if the house collapses in the rains, if the children get sick, and so on.

Yet, is it really worth leaving behind a pretty, simple life, surrounded by friends, family, community, nature, plentiful fruit and fish and *teranga,* to go and live in a cramped room, despised by the local people, working dawn till dusk in the cold, carrying out menial, soul-destroying tasks, in order to send a few quid back to Africa?

I certainly can't blame anyone for trying to better his or her situation. But if they really knew what they were letting themselves in for, I do wonder if so many would still feel it's actually worth risking their life for this Western drudgery.

# AFRICAN ROUGH AND TUMBLE

*We set off from the Gambian border post at Darslami, and within minutes, are lurching through potholes half the depth of Kermit, water washing over the bonnet. I push on, sweating nervously. The rain is pelting down and it's pitch black.*

*We finally arrive at the Senegalese military post. I've been here before at night, and passed without question, but this time four or five heavily-armed soldiers come over, asking what we are doing and where we are going. I tell them we are going to Abéné. They laugh and refute this.*

*"It's too dangerous to drive at night," says the chief. "You won't know the way."*

*I explain that I know the route very well, and that Khady's mother lives in Madina Daffe, a village just three kilometres away. He clearly doesn't believe me, and insists we stay the night.*

*It looks as if we are going to have to sleep in the car, which is filling up with mosquitos, as the windows are wide open. I am already being eaten alive.*

*"This is very difficult," the chief says. "I don't know what we can do. You can't go forward, you can't go back and*

*there's nowhere for you to stay here."*

*When they say something is very difficult with no
solution, that invariably means it's fairly straightforward
and there will be several solutions. You just have to try
and reach one with the shirt still attached to your back.
Normally, as a toubab, I shut up and let the Africans
resolve the situation, but Fitty's only contribution so far
is: "Hey, don't worry; be happy. Yes-aye!"*

This was the final hurdle in a long, drawn-out and tiring
immersion in the rough and tumble of African life. It had
begun when I set off one Saturday morning to collect Kermit
from Brikama, across the border in The Gambia. Years of
scraping through thick bush and hauling logs had left my
trusty Land Rover a little the worse for wear, so I had delivered
him into the care of my mechanic, Amadou Landrover, for a
re-spray.

As Kermit is now an iconic book-cover star, adorning
*Squirting Milk at Chameleons*, I had insisted on retaining the
same shade of vivid green. But you never know what you're
going to get here, and I was a little nervous. I didn't want to
have to change his name to Miss Piggy.

Mr Landrover had told me Kermit would be ready
the following weekend, so I hired the services of my taxi
driver friend, who goes by the name of Allah, to ferry me to
Brikama. My tribulations started when we crossed into The
Gambia to find *set setal* was in progress. We wouldn't be
going anywhere for a couple of hours.

Set means to clean in Wolof, and in fact there's a popular Youssou N'Dour track called "Set" that extols the virtues of keeping your house clean. It seemed such an exotic, otherworldly song until I found out the meaning. *Set setal* is the monthly national cleaning day in The Gambia.

Rather than just keep itself clean on an ongoing basis, the entire country grinds to a halt between 9am and 1pm once a month to pick up litter, and no traffic is allowed on the roads (except perhaps ambulances). It has to be said that The Gambia does now look noticeably cleaner than Senegal, although a recent ban on plastic bags has also helped.

This is one of the differences between democratic Senegal and authoritarian Gambia. Both countries banned plastic around the same time. It hasn't made a blind bit of difference in Senegal, whereas one day after the ban in The Gambia, I was having trouble when buying goods in a supermarket without a bag of my own to hand.

I was slightly wary about entering the country, given recent news. The Gambia's president declared early in 2016, in a move presumably not aimed at attracting more tourists, that his nation is now "the Islamic State of The Gambia". He explained that this was to throw off the final remnants of British colonialism (conveniently ignoring the fact that Islam was brought to West Africa by jihadists during a period of religious wars and resistance against the Arabic colonialists). It's a constant source of bemusement to me that Africans across the continent remain so attached to the religions forced upon them by their colonial oppressors. Apparently, one of the few noticeable changes was that women in government jobs were ordered to wear headscarves. Many didn't like being dictated to like this, so they declined, and barely had the ruling started before it was quietly forgotten about.

When Allah and I eventually rolled into Brikama, I called Amadou Landrover.

"Daddy, definitely Monday…"

I wasn't surprised. I had in fact expected to have to spend a couple of extra days waiting, so I went up to Kololi, at the heart of the tourist "Smiling Coast", to hang out in a café and catch up on some work.

The Gambia's an odd place, but I love it. The vast majority of the country is not very different from Senegal, by which it is almost entirely surrounded. There are the same people, the same tribes and ethnicities, the same landscapes and the same culture and traditions. Communication is much easier for me in The Gambia, however, as most people speak a little English, albeit of a variety that can take some getting used to.

"Big man, boss lady, how's de morning?"

The coastal tourist region is like a different country when compared to the rest of The Gambia, though, resembling a strip of some 1980s semi-developed Mediterranean land, with half-finished cement buildings, hotels, man-made beaches and tourist restaurants selling fish and chips, pizza, Dutch junk food and, of course, gallons of julbrew beer.

Both The Gambia and Senegal are modest and conservative

countries. People, unless labouring, tend to dress smartly, yet it's not so unusual to see big-bellied Brits walking topless, swigging beer in the streets, often accompanied by Gambian girls young enough to be their daughters. The Senegambia "strip" is the epicentre, a metaphorical swamp where, after months in Abéné, I can get a complete and utter culture shock.

Where the bank clerk girls wolf-whistle me and demand my number.

Where the Africell vendor takes my mobile phone number to transfer credit, then, half an hour later, texts to say she's behind on the rent and can I help? If so she'll do anything I ask. And she means anything.

Where the bumsters, usually youngish rasta guys, hustle for business. "Ya alright, big man, lovely jubbly," they declare with exaggerated cockney accents. I try to ignore them but it's hard. I don't want to be rude and ignore everyone, but in a place like this the moment you make eye contact you're in a high-pressure sales negotiation.

Where there is always one *toubab* sitting drunk and sorry having been scammed. The latest one had sent his local wife nearly 30,000 euros to build a house on the land they had purchased, only to find it empty when he arrived back in the country. "Where's the house?" he asked, incredulous and presumably sick to the stomach. "Over there," she said, pointing to the land next door. When I suggested that perhaps she knew the owner of that land, and that this had been the plan all along, I could see the cogs moving.

Where a skinny guy walks up to me declaring "hey, *toubab*, remember me? I'm the guard at your hotel. Lend me some *dalasi* to buy tea. I'll pay you back when you get back." It's a common scam.

Where, when I spot a rat running across the restaurant and point it out to the waiter, he proudly tells me it comes out to play every day.

Where I meet the American guy who's been hanging around for months waiting for a gold (or is it diamond?) deal to come through from Sierra Leone.

Where I overhear British expats who are living here cheaply make comments such as "I've got no time for these people; they're peasants," while the barman is running around trying to keep them happy.

Where the beautiful Liberian girls who could be supermodels in the West, but have been through unspeakable horrors to get here, call out, "Hey mister, let me come go lie with you," in their gentle, lilting, southern States American accents.

There are girls, girls, girls, everywhere, scantily clad in clothes that scream out "come to me, rich *toubab* man," tall, gazelle-like, with tiny waists, and other bits sticking out in all the right places. Oh man, you could get into serious trouble here. For a moment it's highly flattering to have attention from such a beauty, until you see her move on to the old pot-bellied man next to you, and then work her way through the entire bar. And it is not unusual that she will be married, and it is the husband sending her to make money from the *toubabs*.

Of course, it's not all bad, and on a good day I can do Little Baobab to full English fry-up in well under two hours. I can – and often do – have the best of both worlds.

Retreating from Sodom and Gomorrah, I strolled through neighbouring forests, chock-a-block with monkeys, visited the sacred crocodile pool and relaxed on empty beaches. My friend Hami, a *griot kora* player, met me in a café. He was wearing an orange ankle-length *boubou*, his *kora* slung over his shoulder, and sporting trendy shades. The word *griot* is derived from the Portuguese for "troubadour" but that term doesn't adequately describe the meaning. The Mandinka word is *jeli*, which means blood, and you could describe the *griot* as the lifeblood of the culture. They are oral historians, who sing and tell the histories of families at baptisms and other ceremonies. We talked, and then he started to sing, play and tell me legends.

The *kora*, often described as a West African harp, is made from a large, round calabash gourd, from which protrudes a stick strung with 21 strings that make a soft, tinkling, almost classical sound. Hami is tipped to be a star and I had a private audience, which was magical. Tourists across the room tuned in, smiling, nodding along and glimpsing another Africa.

Meanwhile, I was still waiting for news of Kermit. Monday came and went with no joy from Amadou Landrover, but I was assured Kermit would definitely be ready on Tuesday morning.

It was with a certain sense of some relief that I arrived back at Amadou's mango tree at 10am to see Kermit, all spick and span in an almost identical shade to his old colour, and almost new-looking.

"We've just got a few bits to finish off," said Amadou.

"How long will it take?" I asked – one of those questions I know it's a waste of time asking, but do so anyway, albeit with a certain sense of weariness.

"Oh, you'll be out of here at...4pm....*insh'allah*," said with a knowing smile and a shrug.

As good as lounging on the beach in luxury resorts or visiting wildlife sanctuaries might be, by this time, spending the day at a mechanic's workshop seemed a better idea – to keep an eye on proceedings and try to speed them along a little. Amadou operates under some mango trees on the outskirts of Brikama. He excitedly told me he's just taken a second wife, so I'm guessing business must be good, as wives aren't cheap.

I wanted him to take a look at Kermit's brakes, which he duly did. Like mechanics anywhere, though, once he started looking, he found further issues, which I guess is not surprising with a 20-year-old Land Rover that sees some serious off-road action. A small hole in the exhaust was welded over, a universal joint replaced and other bits and pieces fixed, including what is known locally as "the down bit".

I sat there, patiently refusing the multiple offers of *attaya* tea, which is just way too sweet for me. It's always slightly exasperating that I can't leave Amadou to get on with it. Everything has to be watched and monitored, and besides, if he needs something, for example, grease, a boy gets sent to the shop and I have to be on hand to pay. Rather than looking at everything, figuring out what needs to be done and then buying all relevant parts in one go, West African mechanics tackle each job one at a time, with half-hour trips to the spare parts shop between tasks. It might be time for me to come and run a time-management course, although the low cost of getting the parts replaced or fixed kind of makes up for the chaos.

The hours passed slowly. While waiting, I wandered over to the compound of Pa Bobo Jobarteh, which overlooks the "workshop." He's one of The Gambia's top *kora* players, a big star, and is often playing while I'm waiting for the car to be fixed. You could say it's the equivalent of taking your car to Quikfit and popping over for tea with Eric Clapton, who plays for you while you wait. We've known each other a while, and he's keen to come and visit, as well as teach any of our guests interested in this beautiful instrument. This time, he showed me an older CD of his where he's pictured with members of Fairport Convention as they recorded in an English stately home.

"Sherrif (he knows me by my African name), I am good friends with Peter Gabriel. I've made a concert in Singapore. As a boy I was taken to London and played for the Queen, in Buckingham Palace." Given the humble surroundings it seems hard to believe, but it's true – I've seen the pictures.

When I discussed impressions of England with Pa Bobo, he told me he was shocked to see homeless people sleeping on the streets.

"I've never seen that in The Gambia or Casamance, but when I tell my friends here they laugh and think I'm lying, that it can't be true."

Eventually, as dusk fell, three or four days later than advertised, Kermit was finally ready. I took him to pick up some baggage I was bringing for a friend, as well as my slightly annoying buddy Fitty Futta, who'd been buying building materials, and we headed for the border, which is where the problems began again.

I was going the back way, as carrying a lot of baggage through the official route incurs customs fees, and this was just some kitchen gear, clothes and books. The smugglers' route is far simpler, but it does get waterlogged in the rainy season. And, because I never seem to learn, I decided to take the risk.

Which is how we came to be standing around in the pouring rain and the clouds of mosquitos, arguing with the army about being allowed to drive any further. With the resident African still not proffering any solutions, I came up with an idea.

"Look, how about we go and stay with my family in Madina Daffe? I'm certain to catch malaria if I sleep out in the bush."

After much tedious discussion, the chief asked to speak to Khady, presumably to check out my unlikely-seeming story.

I gave him her phone number, so at 10pm she received a call from a soldier asking if she knew Simon Fenton, which obviously terrified her. When he was finally reassured that I did indeed have family in the vicinity, he relented and let us go, making me promise to stop there the night.

We hopped in the car and sped off. As we passed the turning to Madina Daffe, Fitty looked concerned and told me to turn back.

"Hey, don't worry; be happy. Yes-aye!" I told him, and hurried on home, arriving around midnight, exhausted.

As you may be able to tell, I am strangely attached to Kermit, regarding him almost as one of the family. So I was fairly disgruntled when I returned from a trekking trip with guests to find part of his back panelling ripped off, dents in his side and bonnet, a wing mirror hanging off and a back light smashed.

Khady had been in Ziguinchor and I'd made the mistake of leaving the key behind. It took some while for the true story as to how this had happened to be uncovered; rumours eventually surfaced of Fakeba "boy racing" around Abéné in Kermit, revealing also that he had lied to us about the cause of the damage.

Interestingly, though Khady was as angry with Fakeba as I was, the focus of her anger was on the fact that he had lied. The fact that he'd taken and crashed the car clearly seemed trivial to her – and to other friends I spoke to about it. Belongings – even expensive ones – don't seem to be that important here. They're "just stuff".

This casual attitude to private property is a not-infrequent source of my feelings that life – and people – can treat me (or/and my things) roughly here. Perhaps it's because traditional items are so durable, and everything else is cheap Chinese crap that only lasts five minutes anyway.

Whatever the cause, the fact remains that many of my things get broken – often apparently without contrition or concern. Like when Fakeba decided to jam my expensive chef's knife into a coconut and snapped it. Or Yama carelessly placed my French glass cafetière half on and half off the table – with inevitable consequences. It's not so much the loss itself that irks me, but the fact that I can't easily replace the item, and that I had gone to the trouble of shipping it all the way here.

Everything breaks, nothing lasts and I'm starting to regret bringing anything of value. Books rot or are eaten by termites; clothes are coated in a fine dust of fungus; the two tablets I bought for Khady, along with multiple phones, lasted, at most, a few weeks. The combination of tiled floors, kids and electronics is not a happy one.

I am slowly letting go. My computer and my camera are lifelines to my work, but aside from these...well, as Khady says, it's just stuff.

"Will you take it when you die?" she asks me, every time another of my favourite coffee mugs that I've had for 25 years is smashed. Well, no, but that doesn't mean I can't say "grrr" and shake my fist a little.

One of my worst losses was when I was clambering on rocks by the ocean to take a sunset photo. I lost my footing on the slippery stone and went down headfirst onto a rock before rolling over into the sea, camera first. I placed the camera in a sack of rice for more than a week – a recommended course of action to dry it out – but it showed no sign of recovery. It's just stuff, Simon; it's just stuff. Expensive stuff, mind.

The damage to Kermit on that occasion was, in the end, fairly superficial, but he's well on the way to becoming a fully Africanised vehicle now; not exactly a possession I can be too proud of any longer.

I think the oddest example I saw of the Africanisation of a car was in the east of the country. The driver had a curious method of switching off the engine. He'd turn and remove the key, at which point the engine continued to run. There was a length of rubber tubing poking out of a gap near the ignition keyhole. He inserted this into his mouth, blew hard and the engine closed down.

Another badly Africanised vehicle that had particularly unhappy consequences for me was a wrecked old bush taxi I once travelled in on the way back from Ziguinchor. There was a massive storm along the way, and, as usual, the bush taxi leaked, so I had a constant drip of water on my shoulder. After a while, I realised it was no longer raining – but I was still getting wet. I then realised the liquid had a pungent goaty smell. Yes, there were a couple of sheep tied to the roof, and I was getting pissed on.

More everyday African rough and tumble.

Somewhat more extreme was another (mis-)adventure into the forest near Madina Daffe. This one was supposed to be a quick turnaround with Khady to pick up a few sacks of charcoal from the house of a *marabout* and alleged former rebel fighter. We tended to cook on charcoal before we built a rocket stove, and this was considerably cheaper than buying charcoal in Abéné. We were also preparing for a biannual visit by Overlanding West Africa, a tour group of around 20 people from all over the world, who were about to camp on our land.

The rains seemed to have finished and the land had started drying out, which would make it easier for them to pitch tents, but then, just before they arrived, there were two more days of torrential rains, and the road to our place became a swamp. I started shovelling sand into old rice sacks and making sandbag stepping stones.

Then we went to pick up the charcoal. Driving through potholes that are so deep you can feel the car slipping down the sides is exhilarating – but scary. As we drove, I thought, "I probably shouldn't be risking this the day before a large group arrives. What if we break down and get stuck out here?"

As so often happens when I have such thoughts, I promptly stalled. Where are those hornbills when you need them? I hadn't seen one for a long time and I sure could have used an injection of luck. I tried to start the engine and heard only a grinding sound. I thought there was water in the electrical system so, when a crowd of kids inevitably arrived, we managed to push Kermit out onto a flat surface, where they attempted to push-start me. It was probably the worst thing I could have done.

There was no joy, so I went to call the trusty Omar to ask for help, but my phone was dead. Khady's – typically – had no credit, so we were stuck in the swamp forest, wondering what to do next. I was mentally thinking of all the jobs I needed to complete before my 20 guests arrived. "Feeling slightly anxious" would be an understatement of my condition.

We were just a couple of kilometres from Madina Daffe, so I suggested to Khady that we walk back there, but she was feeling too sick and weak to walk. There was nothing for it but to carry her. She had been suffering from what sounded like heartburn as well as headaches for some time. We'd been to many clinics, both local and international-quality, but no one had been able to properly diagnose the issue.

As luck would have it, Madina does have a small village clinic. On my first ever visit to the village, I had been driving along the torturous, potholed, jungle track when we picked up a man dressed more or less in rags. It turned out he was the doctor of the clinic. Khady's sister Sire was also the pharmacist there, and had given birth to her baby, Simon Fenton Deidhou in the clinic.

I struggled on through the dank, humid heat, my flipflops sliding in the slimy mud, half-staggering and half-carrying Khady, who was slipping in and out of consciousness.

We arrived an hour or so later, sweating and exhausted. The raggedly attired chap, Famara Sanya, was in his white doctor's jacket this time, and rapidly saw to Khady, while I gave my phone batteries a quick boost with the hospital solar system, and bought some credit.

Khady had been convinced this doctor would help with her problems, but once again she was merely prescribed ampicillin, paracetamol and vitamin C – things that seem to get prescribed here for any and every issue. After a rest and some tea, she did perk up though.

Famara and Sire explained that they have never received any government assistance or funding. They don't receive a salary either. They have built and run the place entirely with donations from local villagers. Given the levels of poverty, they've done a good job, although to anyone looking with Western eyes, it has nothing: a simple concrete structure, an inefficient solar system (the nearest electricity line is about 18 kilometres away), ramshackle beds, insect-ridden ceilings and a poorly-stocked drugs cupboard.

This lack of governmental support doesn't surprise me, but it seems incomprehensible when you see the projects that *are* supported. There's currently a programme to build a concrete wall around village football pitches, for example. Abéné had a beautiful football field, a picturesque clearing amid tall jungle trees and palms. Now it has a concrete wall that cost millions of francs and will be black and mouldy within a year or two in the tropical humidity, like all the other half-finished concrete walls that are increasingly cluttering Abéné. The ostensible purpose is to be able to control spectators coming in, and charge them a few coins. Well, they used to build a palm-leaf natural fence and do the same thing. Meanwhile, the local school doesn't even have toilets, and villages like Madina have to build their own clinics, or, as with Abéné and other places frequented by whites, obtain funding from a philanthropic *toubab*.

Madina clinic needs maintenance, cleaning products, drugs, medical equipment and, I'm sure, much more. Famara told me that a woman had come in to give birth the previous day but there were complications they couldn't deal with. She was put on the back of a motorbike to go to the nearest hospital – a woman halfway through childbirth had to travel 18 kilometres on bumpy, pothole-ridden, swampy jungle track. Neither she nor the baby made it.

It seemed to me that Famara and his team were motivated and talented, but limited by circumstances. He explained he'd been here several years now, as he wants to help, but he could have got a paid posting in Ziguinchor or Dakar. He's not sure how much longer he can continue; he has a family to feed, after all. And I guess that, like others here, he survives by subsistence farming and odd jobs on top of the medical work.

The small donations I make when I visit the village with guests are just drops in the ocean; clearly not a long-term solution. My hope is that by being part of a community that builds businesses, attracts tourists to the region, supports entrepreneurs such as Khady, employs local people and puts money back into the local economy, I can do my small bit to help the region develop sustainably.

money back into the local economy, I can do my small bit to help the region develop sustainably.

Finally I had some battery charge and some credit. One thing was still missing: reception. I could only wait, so I sat with a tired Khady and played with young Simon Fenton Deidhou. Thankfully, within the hour a bar appeared on the phone and I was able to call Omar. He turned up a couple of hours later and we headed back to Kermit.

He took a brief look and uttered those dreaded words: "It's the timing belt." If that doesn't mean much to you, check with someone mechanically minded and watch their reaction. I'd only replaced my timing belt a few months earlier and was under the impression its timing should be considerably longer-term.

"Well, this is Africa," said Omar. Maybe, but it still felt unlucky – unluckier than the last time the belt had gone.

I'd travelled upcountry to Janjanbureh and the River Gambia national park to view chimpanzees with Mart, one of my regular guests. The timing belt had broken on the return drive, but we'd been relatively lucky. A bus had towed us the 100 km or so to Brikama, where we transferred smoothly to a private car and were back at the Little Baobab before you could say "Let's drink sun-downers on the terrace."

This African rough and tumble is pretty constant, but it's rarely catastrophic and it's all part of the fun – at least, retrospectively. After all, if I wanted an easy time of it, I could have stayed in England. I enjoy visiting the UK, but I am always eager to get back here. The beauty and adventure of my African life easily outweigh the discomforts and problems.

Mind you, it's now getting to the point where every time I get into Kermit I am unsure whether I'll get home again, which is a bit stressful. On this occasion, it turned out that although Omar had come on a bike and without a tow rope, a friend of his who lived nearby was able to tow us the 30 kilometres home, for a sum of money that wouldn't buy a small round of drinks in London. We even managed to pick up the charcoal, arriving, to Gulliver's delight, as darkness fell. And I still had half a day to get everything ready for Overlanding West Africa.

Despite – or perhaps because of? – the undoubted toughness of life in Africa, I find I usually feel really happy here. I won't or can't ignore the world's injustices and sorrows – and I see a fair few of them here – but I refuse to let them get me down (that's not going to help anyone, after all). I keep my focus instead on all the joys and wonders of daily life.

Just weeks after I was playing with him in Madina Daffe, we heard that young Simon Fenton Deidhou had passed away. Nobody knew why. Rough and tumble.

# EXOTIC AFFLICTIONS

*You know that feeling when something seems to be crawling about inside your skull, right? The pain is fierce and I've been gulping painkillers for weeks. The already huge boil on the hairline of my forehead is growing larger by the day and bloody pus leaks on to my pillow every night.*

*Despite Khady's demands not to touch it, I can wait no longer and decide, despite the agony, to crush out the poison. As I grit my teeth, thick yellow discharge trickles into my eyes, but one congealed chunk eludes me. With tweezers, I gently prod and, with a slurping sound that will forever haunt me, out it pops, leaving clear red liquid pulsating out of the swollen hole in my head.*

*Then, as I look closely I am astonished to see it isn't a clotted lump.*

*It is a still-wriggling maggot.*

Health is perhaps one of my biggest concerns, especially now that I'm responsible for a young family. Until this point, I'd winged it. Local healthcare is cheap and, while I was constantly prescribed the same medicines, with a biology degree and a couple of decent medical manuals, I thought

I could cope. Besides, local doctors are probably a better bet for treating the common tropical diseases. I'm constantly amazed by how many tourists are taking anti-malarial medications prescribed by Western GPs that are deemed out of date and ineffective here .

But the maggot in my forehead almost had me throwing in the towel. As a boy I'd always fancied an action man-style facial scar. I don't think I'd ever envisioned it being caused by a maggot. It was the larva of a tumba fly, which lays its eggs in washing hung out to dry during the rainy season. The only explanation I can think of for the larva's presence on my forehead is that my towel had received the unwanted attentions of a broody fly. I don't tend to wear a hat.

There is actually a simple preventive measure; Khady has bought an iron, so all washed clothes will be pressed in future, to kill any eggs. As we can't power anything with a heating element using our solar power system, she uses the type of iron that we Europeans must have used in the 19th century. It's an old-fashioned metal contraption, into which you insert lumps of red-hot charcoal.

Rainy season is always difficult, medically speaking. Months on end of damp, humid and hot weather mean that minor wounds become infected and, if you're not very careful, they don't dry out and heal. Each year I have managed to contract some kind of lurgy, and each year I have told myself, "Okay, I'm steadily becoming acclimatised," only to find myself with a worse problem the following year.

Last year, I was halfway through watching an episode of

*Downton Abbey* when I convinced myself I had elephantiasis. Watching this British Sunday night comfort telly on my laptop is a guilty pleasure – one that also feels a little surreal in monsoonal West Africa. The show is filmed close to my parents' home, and I'm afraid that by watching it with Khady I might have set up some false expectations for her when she finally visits England. Although I've explained to her that I am in fact descended from the servant classes, even life below stairs looks like luxury to your typical African villager.

So anyway, there I was, deeply absorbed in the 1920s class system, when I hit the pause button, as my foot was, as the Gambians say, "paining me." Flicking through a medical text to try to get to the source of the problem, I came across an article: "Six parasites you definitely don't want to host."

It turned out I'd already had three of them, and that a fourth, filarial worm, sounded exactly like whatever was infecting my foot. It started as an itch between the two smallest toes on my right foot. A day later, the itching was intense and it felt like someone had smashed the side of my foot with a sledge-hammer.

Khady called it by the Diola name, *polinka*, and squeezed the boiling juice from a local fruit, baked on the fire, onto the affected area, which was nice. There was relief for a few days until all the skin from the toe was shed, leaving a raw open wound that oozed pus for about a month.

Before this puts you off visiting, first, you can only catch this in the rainy season and second, you would have to be a chump like me who wanders around barefoot. Everyone warned me not to do this (I only do it in my garden), but I didn't listen, thinking they were just concerned about thorns in my foot. My soles are pretty tough now. No one mentioned the *polinka*.

I had thought my symptoms matched those of the dreaded filarial worm, which can lead to elephantiasis, the condition John Merrick, the so-called Elephant Man, suffered from. Although I enjoyed the film and read his biography, I hadn't wanted to take my interest that far. Luckily, it turned out that *polinka*, while agonisingly painful and somewhat inconvenient, didn't have such serious consequences. I've tried to get an English or French translation for the *polinka* without success. All I've discovered is that there are many such parasites and creepy-crawlies that don't have translations, as Europeans don't generally suffer from them. Clearly I'm special.

More recently, a small insect bite on my cheek became infected, swelled up, throbbed and kept me awake for several nights. With my face significantly distended, this time I really did look like the elephant man. I don't know if the infection spread or if it was just the season for it, but a couple of mosquito bites on my leg also became infected, and looked like bullet wounds. There were actual holes in my calf. Before I'd looked and realised how bad it was, I went to scratch the bite with my finger and it sank into what felt like a bowl of warm rice pudding. Fakeba is well used to such diseases, and brings me handfuls of local herbs and leaves, with which he tenderly cleans the wounds and attaches a poultice to draw out all the pus and poison.

When we first received Ketchup, our new puppy, I spent a few days squeezing mango worms and picking off ticks. The worms are buried in the skin, usually around the dog's paws and ears and on its tail. A quick squeeze pops them out – wriggling maggots about half a centimetre in length. All African dogs seem to suffer from them. They're quite nutritious (no I haven't tried them, in case you are wondering) and the chickens arrive on the scene pretty quickly whenever I'm popping them out onto the floor.

Ketchup wasn't the only one with a worm. I cut my toenails one day and didn't see anything unusual. The next day, I noticed my little toe nail was black. Closer inspection showed that it appeared to be decomposing and surrounded by inflamed skin, seemingly filled with pus. I took a needle for a rummage and quickly pulled out a couple of wriggling worms and plenty of eggs. I'd spent a fair bit of time in Christian Diola villages around this period, and they tend to be full of pigs, which are notorious for these chiggers.

Once I was certain I'd removed all the eggs, Khady doused it with petrol and I set it alight (the latter bit's not strictly true, but the petrol does kill them), in case there were any more. Luckily I'd found them in time. Any longer and I'd certainly have lost the nail, and possibly the toe. Talking of which, a couple of days later I was swinging from a rope in one of my trees (hey, I'm in Africa; this is what I do) when I slipped and broke a toe, which left me feeling a bit of a prat.

Undeterred, I carried on thinking that things can only get

better. A little later in the rainy season, I found myself back in The Gambia, having Kermit serviced under another mango tree.

One evening I returned to my hotel about midnight, having had only a couple of beers, so I couldn't even blame my stupidity on booze. The gates were closed and there was no security guard in sight. After banging and hollering, I decided to go over the wall.

I climbed up and then put my hand down and vaulted over. As something warm and wet sprayed over me, I realised I'd placed my hand on jagged glass embedded there to stop plonkers like me from jumping over. Blood was gushing out and I saw that my hand was split in two.

There was no one to help, and this being The Gambia, there was no running water in my room, so I wrapped my hand in a sock and fell asleep. When I awoke some hours later, hand throbbing, it looked as if I was on the set of a slasher movie. Blood was sprayed all over the floor tiles and formed a trail all the way to the wall I'd jumped over.

There was a clinic nearby where a nurse cleaned the wound with alcohol, a little more enthusiastically than I'd have wished for, then sewed it up with seven stitches.

Given that she'd recently given birth to two children, I didn't dare milk too much sympathy from Khady. My hand healed well – no mean feat in the hot, humid rainy season – but there was a problem. When the stitches were removed, I realised the finger was stuck in a bent position and that I was unable to stretch my hand out. I was perpetually beckoning someone. I returned to the clinic and was put in touch with a doctor from Sierra Leone, supposedly one of the best neurosurgeons in West Africa, who explained that he would cut it open, stretch the finger out and splint it in the stretched-out position.

I had thought it would be a simple process, but found myself getting dressed up in green overalls and being wheeled on a trolley into a rather dark, rundown operating theatre, as a team of people in masks loomed over me, telling me not to worry. As scenes from the slasher movie, *Saw*, ran through my head, I just shut my eyes, gritted my teeth and tried to remember that this was the best neurosurgeon in West Africa.

There was one positive side effect: I was unable to put my hand in my pocket to remove money, which, given that it was the Islamic Tabaski holiday and there were many expenses, was quite useful.

The relentless illnesses, infections and infestations have at times made me question whether I can really survive all year round in Senegal. At first I didn't take them too seriously. Despite occasionally excruciating pain, I'd laugh, take a photo to gross out my patient and long-suffering friends, and tell everyone that I had another great story to tell. Moreover, I receive a lot of love. Sometimes when she thinks I'm asleep, I feel Khady investigating my feet for worms by torch-light. That's true love, that is.

But many other *toubabs* return to Europe for the rainy

season, which may just be a better idea. After all, in Abéné we have near-perfect weather from about November through till June. One could return to the UK for a pleasant European summer, enjoy a little autumn and then head back to hammock land for the cold bit.

That's easier said than done with a family, though, and it still seems to me like cheating. Aside from anything else, we have been developing a thriving tourist business, which is starting to keep us busy even during the low season. And in many ways, the rainy season is my favourite time of year, as everything glistens green, the atmosphere when clear is a photographer's dream, and it's quiet, as most *toubabs* – and even many Africans – leave the village. But it sure is hell at times for heat, humidity, insects and disease.

And I'm not the only one who has been afflicted by health problems. Khady was still suffering from chest pains and headaches, latterly diagnosed as anaemia, although the iron she was given didn't help and still the pain continued. Also, one day we noticed a small swelling in Gulliver's groin.

Local doctors gave the usual prescription of ampicillin, paracetamol and vitamin C, while scaring Khady by telling her how serious it was and that he would have to go to Europe for surgery. I told her we should get a second opinion, and that, no, I wasn't being tight with money by not bothering with the drugs, but these things are always prescribed when local doctors don't understand the problem. And often when they do understand, because they like to cover all bases.

Following my surgical experience, I'd made a serious effort

to find decent local medical facilities, and I'd discovered a brand new European-style hospital just over the border in The Gambia. I was reassured by British-trained Indian surgeons and a Swiss doctor there that although surgery was required for Gulliver's groin, it was a very minor procedure (and not at all unusual), and that they were fully qualified to do it. It's reassuring to have a high-quality facility just 50 kilometres from home.

I later returned with Gully. Khady stayed at home, as she thought she'd be too traumatised. He wasn't allowed to eat or drink beforehand, so I managed to get him, still sleeping, into a bed set up in the back seat of Kermit. As any parent will understand, watching him being taken into the operating theatre was distressing; he's the monkey boy, a free-range kid who plays in the forest every day. I'll never forget the look of absolute terror on his face as the nurse carried him screaming from my arms and into the theatre.

"You're supposed to protect me," was what his eyes told me as I dissolved inside, trying not to cry.

It was all over very quickly and they said it was a textbook op. He slept for several hours, connected to a drip – another thing that is distressing for any parent to see – and then curled up in the back of Kermit as we drove back through the bush.

The next day, he proudly pointed at his bandage, said "*buco-buco*" (it hurts) then ran away and did a cartwheel. Khady and I jumped out of our chairs, but he was clearly back to normal and all was fine.

After the operation I bought Gulliver some toys, including

a wooden Pinocchio puppet. As he played with it I explained to Khady the story of the little wooden boy whose nose grew larger if he told lies. Unbelievably, a few days later I had an infection inside my nostril, and another tropical boil swelled painfully, turning the end of my normally petit schnoz into a swollen clown-like monstrosity that prompted me to wander around painfully, humming "Rudolph the red-nosed reindeer" to myself.

It also caused me a massive problem with Khady, who was convinced that I must be telling porkies.

Still, I now knew we had a good hospital within easy reach, and was beginning to feel more confident about healthcare issues. Then Ebola struck.

In contrast with the slew of scare stories across the Western media, there was not much publicity about the disease locally. I started seeing notices at the Senegal-Gambia border, and after shaking my hand, the immigration guys would point me towards huge containers of disinfectant so I could wash my hands.

Life carried on, and while some *toubabs* would humorously raise their hand, stating "Ebola" rather than performing the traditional shake, locals continued to shake hands normally, and to eat communally from large rice bowls. Although hundreds of kilometres from infected regions, we do share a border with Guinea. The Senegal health authorities are far more developed than those in Guinea, Sierra Leone and

Liberia. There was one reported case of Ebola in Dakar, Senegal, when a Guinean student, already infected, decided to cross the closed border. The authorities traced his route and quarantined everybody who'd been in contact with him. The infection went no further.

After a headache you get a fever, then your immune system throws in the towel, your guts fill with blood and you leak blood from your eyes, nose, mouth and anus. Then you die and your body melts and turns to slime. If someone scrapes you up to bury you, they will be infected. No vaccine, no cure. No wonder it freaked everyone out.

Yes, Ebola is a horrible disease, but it's highly unlikely that you'll catch it unless working with infected patients or their dead bodies. A bit of perspective: there were just over 11,000 deaths from Ebola between the time of outbreak and the end of 2015. This is across a vast region with a population of more than 340 million.

It might sound a lot, but the human brain and the modern media are notoriously bad at analysing risk, a fact often trotted out when people worry about air travel versus roads. According to WHO, the common flu claims on average, 250,000 to 500,000 lives per year, worldwide.

Many also believe that the numbers were being hyped to maximise foreign donations. And who supplies the numbers? The remote African hospitals and African governments – organisations hardly known for their efficiency.

But it's tragic that something affecting a small area has devastated an entire region. I even heard that people were avoiding Tanzania, and that tourism was reduced as far afield as South Africa. The affected countries are closer to London than to Tanzania. Can you imagine the uproar if Americans cancelled trips to the UK because of an outbreak of bird flu in Greece? I certainly don't blame people in infected regions from panicking, but for the majority of us, surely a sense of perspective is required.

One would-be guest certainly understood this; during the outbreak I received this email: "Simon, there's more Ebola here in New York City than in Senegal. Will you still allow us to visit?"

It seems to me there is always heightened fear and paranoia in the media where Africa is concerned and, despite Africa being a continent of more than 50 countries, and countless ethnicities, languages and cultures, with plenty of success stories, it never seems to take long for the "dark continent" narrative to re-emerge whenever there's a crisis.

Which is unfortunate as, to me, Africa projects warmth and welcome and light. Except when it's throwing maggots my way.

# LIVING WITH SPIRITS

*I am up to my neck in a river, hoping the crocodiles aren't hungry, and waiting in line with Khady and 20 other local people. Khady has insisted that we go through this ceremony before I take a trip. The magical protection provided will surely bring us luck and protect us from evil forces.*

*Earlier we'd gone to the home of an old witch – sorry, I mean an old "spiritual lady" – who, with a toothless grin, led us down to the river...*

*A bunch of old women tend the fetish; a smoothed tree stump at the base of a sacred tree. It is well swept and covered in offerings such as sweets, biscuits, cigarettes and milk. I am told to strip down to my shorts and enter the river. We all crouch down, water to our shoulders, eyes closed and think about what we want in life. Then we swim (at least I do) or wade (African's don't do swimming) downstream to an archway of wood that barely protrudes from the water's surface. One at a time we approach the arch, make our wish again and dive through it, three times each. Not a problem for me but everyone else coughs and splutters.*

*Next we sit by the fetish shrine. Khady can sit all day on the floor, back straight, legs outstretched. Me? Two minutes is more than enough. The ants are vicious and I am left itching for days. Each of us pays our fee and then the old ladies chant our names and wishes.*

*As I leave, I am dragged into a palm-leaf cubicle where another old granny ladles green leafy liquid all over me and makes me drink some of the slimy but sweet liquid.*

*Khady and I are well and truly protected. Apparently.*

It was the time of the *harmattan*, the constant wind that blows down from the deserts of the north, giving the landscape an otherworldly hazy glow as the sun appeared twice its normal size and hung low in the sky. All of my plants and trees were covered with a fine dusting of Saharan sand and everyone seemed to be coughing and spluttering, their throats clogged.

But we're not in the UK and I can't remember ever discussing the weather with Khady. Over another plate of rice and fish, she said, in our peculiar French-English creole: "C'est necessary you help me more, me I faire toute."

I was shattered after a week of backbreaking labour in the hot and dusty garden, building raised permaculture compost beds.

"What? Every day I'm working and then writing. How do you think we get guests to come here?"

"Bollocks!" – an ancient Senegalese phrase she's fond of – "I protected the land, the *marabouts* helped you, and without the spirits we'd have nothing."

I think she was being facetious, knowing I'm busy every day, but I also know she thinks that without the spiritual protection, we'd be finished. And she's probably right. I couldn't live here without her, and if she wasn't convinced we were sufficiently protected with *gris-gris* and so on, then I've no doubt she wouldn't survive – and I mean that literally.

Whatever my beliefs, I try to respect hers but I do have to challenge her when something seems to me to be completely ridiculous. For example, I was painting the walls in our bedroom and pointed something out to Khady: every room has a grubby patch near the light switch, where people with dirty hands have groped the wall looking for the switch. I'd understand if it was the kids but they can't reach these switches.

"You know why this is?" said Khady. "We like to have a dirty patch near the light switch. If we have a sore throat, we'll lick these dirty bits and then a few days later we'll be better."

I really did think I'd heard it all, but that was truly brilliant.

Then there was the day Alfie's scalp was a little flaky. I suggested she use a little moisturiser but Khady had a better idea: "We can take the contents of a freshly killed sheep's stomach and plaster that all over his head," she suggested.

Fair enough, perhaps I'll pass the formula on to Head & Shoulders, the popular British anti-dandruff shampoo. Well, it did work. And come on, you've got to admit it, this beats talking about the weather, right?

Still, Khady felt I wasn't taking her beliefs seriously, and wanted to bring another *marabout* to the house. In her opinion, our various businesses weren't progressing fast enough and we needed a little spiritual help. The *marabout* subsequently arrived and gave us some prayer scrolls, one for each corner of the land and another for the dead centre of it. We had to bury them. These were in order to bring luck for my writing career. Far more important, Khady thought, than my own relentless internet promotion.

The *marabouts* are like mechanics. They come to sort out one problem and then point out a bunch more. This time it was our *fromager* trees. In the Diola and other local animistic traditions, large trees, especially *fromagers*, or kapok, of which we have six or so on our land, are haunted or protected, depending upon your viewpoint, by a genie. This is supposedly some kind of spirit that may be good or bad.

The *marabout* provided some instructions and Khady set up a small shrine to the genie: a *jalang* (a powerful *gris-gris*), an old painted turtle shell she found on the beach and a couple of woodcarvings. Every Friday, she sweeps the area, and occasionally pours some palm wine at the base of the tree.

I'm a stranger in a strange land. I try to understand, I try to respect Khady's beliefs and I'd gone along with making the shrine, but occasionally I may be guilty of letting a little scepticism shine through.

"You really believe there's a genie?"

She was insistent that genies do exist, and that the marabout could show one to me, thus providing me with proof.

"Okay, you're on," I said. Despite my rational response of believing it to be nonsense, a chill ran down my spine. This is Africa; it is very dark, and there are many things I'll never understand.

Khady wandered off to the *marabout* and he agreed to introduce me to the male genie. He says there is also a female one but she's far too dangerous and I could die if I'm not careful. As it is, if I'm not strong I could go mad. Khady explained the genie could be revealed to me, but in return I would need to make a sacrifice.

And there I was, hoping he'd offer three wishes.

"Sacrifice? You mean a chicken or a goat?"

"Probably, but it could also be a person. If you don't offer a name, the genie will kill you."

A couple of folk sprang to mind but I joked and said, "Okay, we can sacrifice you."

That was the wrong thing to say. Khady immediately looked terrified and said, "No, no, we can't do this. You're not serious, you don't believe me. I'm scared now."

It was stupid and naive of me to make jokes of this nature and I instantly regretted it. It's a bit like magic tricks. You must take care if performing these in some remoter parts of Africa, as you can be accused of witchcraft.

Right after this conversation, Khady started putting charcoal on the window sill, which is a well-known genie-deterrent in these parts. She also gave Gulliver and Alfie extra *gris-gris*, leaving me feeling pretty uneasy. After all, I was bringing them up here for the quality of life. It's all very well living in such an idyllic paradise, but was it going to be dangerous? Were my children going to believe all of this and be unable to adapt to a Western mentality, should they decide to go there? I was starting to flit back and forth, unsure of whether I was doing the right thing. It would surely be all right in the end, wouldn't it?

I have absolutely no doubt that there will not be a genie but I'm obliged to choose a person to die – or I myself will die if there actually is a genie? Hmmm, now that's not a scenario I ever envisaged myself being in, to be honest. Then again, I never thought the mother of my children would be squirting breast milk at chameleons; that I'd be holed up in someone's house with terrified people as a red furry masked creature clanged machetes outside; that our ex-electrician would bloat up and die from a curse, having been accused of stealing a cow; that I myself would receive jolting pains down my back rendering me immobile after shaking hands with a woman who had supposedly cursed me; that I'd enjoy watching the Chadian version of *X-Factor*. Life is full of surprises, and that's why I'm here.

Later, the *marabout* returned, much to my surprise, given the conversation with Khady. He's about half my age and owns around half the number of teeth that I possess. He seemed impressed by my Diola and possibly more impressed by the large hunting knife that hung from the belt of my shorts. After some conversation he gave his terms and then disappeared into the forest to gather the necessary materials for the great genie reveal.

Given the choice between a rational explanation or a supernatural one, I've noticed many Africans (and non-Africans, to be fair) will choose the supernatural. Although most "mystic African" things seemed fairly explicable to me, I still continued to have some weird experiences.

If I wasn't of sound scientific education, if I didn't know there are many things we don't understand for which science may uncover a rational explanation at some point in the future, then perhaps I could quite easily be drawn into becoming more superstitious.

The thing I struggled to understand is that if everyone is so busy protecting themselves, casting spells and consulting miracle-performing marabouts, then why aren't these people the strongest, most powerful people and nations on the planet? I've never received a response to that question – just bafflement as to why I'd even ask it.

Sometimes this belief in the power of *gris-gris* does go too far. One young chap I heard about was so eager to test his new protective gris-gris' magical powers that he threw a spear up into the air and let it fall back down straight into himself, believing he was invincible. Perhaps the *ju-ju* just wasn't strong enough, as the spear returned to earth straight through his eye socket, blinding him.

Despite my scepticism, I've seen a few things here that have freaked me out, and for which I've not found an explanation, unless someone was deliberately messing with me, which seems unlikely, as most local people are terrified of the supernatural and wouldn't joke about it.

The first scary experience was during the Abéné festival about three years ago. I was attending every performance and taking photographs for the organisers, and usually it was the small hours before the performance would wind up. As I've often remarked, I never feel any sense of danger in Abéné and am quite happy to walk alone at any hour.

So upon leaving one evening at around 2am, I was walking home alone down a dark sandy track. It was a little misty and the moon was full, so the light was diffused but bright and I had no need for a torch. Nearing our place, I passed a large tree where I caught a glimpse of something. I turned and was a little perturbed to see a figure in a robe with a hood pulled up and standing still with his or her arms slightly outstretched and dangling down. I couldn't see a face, muttered "bonsoir" to no response and carried on, feeling uneasy. After a few seconds I turned back but there was no one there. So, despite being a fully-grown 40-something-year-old man, I ran home.

About a week later I was walking home by a different route, across a piece of wetland between our house and the beach. I was halfway across when I had that uneasy feeling of someone watching me. I turned and looked back to see a similar-looking hooded figure, about 100 metres away on the edge of the forest, again, standing stock still. Quickening my pace, I marched forward, turning back about five seconds later, to see that the figure was now only about 20 metres behind me. Once again I broke into a run and turned, but could see nothing there. Was it my imagination? A trick of the light? Who knows?

I am still sure there must be a rational explanation, although I'm darned if I know what it is. Perhaps now is the time to explain a ghost story from my home town during my teenage years. There was a leisure centre there called the Old Gaol. It was several hundred years old and had indeed once been a prison. Legend had it that hangings had taken place there and, inevitably, it was thought to be haunted.

Eventually some proof came along when a cleaner arrived at 4am and caught sight of a ghostly figure on the balcony of the swimming pool at the centre. She ran scared, but returned with somebody else, to find nothing and no one there. This story was reported in the local newspaper that week and there the story ended.

I can now reveal that I had been working as a lifeguard at that pool and, following a staff party, went for a lie down. A combination of Strongbow cider and warm chlorine-infused air caused me to fall fast asleep, until I was rudely awakened by a cleaner screaming at me at 4 in the morning.

Still I was waiting to see the genie, and I asked Khady what was going on. Where was the *marabout*?

"He is in the forest, summoning the spirits."

In the meantime, Khady had decided she needed medicine for a herbal shower, which was available from another *marabout* in Madina Daffe. Spiritual protection never ends.

We arrived in time to eat some chicken and greasy rice with her mother. We all crouched around a central platter and ate with our hands. It'll be a while before I can introduce my kids into polite society.

Talking of which, in the UK you might take your mother-in-law a bunch of flowers or box of chocolates, but here I'm more inclined to take a sack of cement so she can mend the floor. Once, when I was staying at her place, I stepped out of bed and the mud floor collapsed beneath my feet, as there had been so much termite activity below the surface.

There was no moon and no electricity, so we sat in the pitch black and chatted, before an early night. Khady's mother told me how life had changed in the past 30 years.

"Everyone wore rags, no one could afford pets and we hardly ever ate fish or meat. When we did, we'd even eat the bones."

Life is improving slowly and although still poor, Aida Mane now eats fish most days, has a mobile phone, dresses in beautiful brightly patterned African cloths and has a couple of dogs sitting at her feet. She could even visit the neighbours to watch television, although she doesn't, preferring the old ways.

So why is it that so many of the younger generations are risking it all to go to Libya and get to Europe? As usual, Khady has a theory.

"Before, we didn't have televisions, but now we do, we can see the whole world, and some people even have internet. Now we know what the *toubab* has. The Africans helped build America, but not by choice. Can you blame us for wanting some of the West's riches?"

This increased interaction with the wider world, as well as the opportunities and routes opened up as a result of the current anarchy in Libya, are major reasons why people are heading for the West now, when their much poorer parents and grandparents didn't.

I kept a lookout for Khady's cousin Insa, but he was nowhere to be seen. I asked a few people where he was but I received only vacant shrugs. I think they knew, but they weren't going to tell me.

After the meal, a peddler showed up, selling clothes and goods off his bicycle, which he pushes from village to village. One teenage girl hanging out there wanted me to buy her some skin-whitening cream. I told her this was not good, and refused, but I think she thought I was just being mean, and wandered off, muttering something that sounded very much like "you wait, *toubab*." Despite her youth and innocent looks, the look on her face had me spooked.

Everyone else seemed pleased to see me, and I felt privileged when Khady's brother Mustafa invited me to see a ceremony later that evening involving knife-cutting, one of the more secretive Diola practices. Dancers, protected by herbal concoctions and plenty of *gris-gris*, slice themselves with razor-sharp knives but, because of the magical protection, their skin remains unbroken.

The ceremony was to send off boys who were heading into the forest for their initiation ceremony. I arrived to see a big circle of clickety-clackety women beneath some mango and cashew trees. That is my affectionate name for the Diola women who stand in a circle at ceremonies banging together either two bits of wood or two bits of metal in a highly rhythmic manner.

A group of men and boys danced in circles, some occasionally breaking out into what I call the Diola flap. This consists of bending the body so that the back is at about a 90-degree angle to the legs, while staring straight ahead and stretching the arms out to the sides. The hands then appear to massage the head of an imaginary small person, while the legs stamp up and down on the spot as if trying to put out a vigorously burning fire.

Mustafa himself danced into a trance-like frenzy, then took a knife and viciously sliced his arms and neck with a manic expression on his face. In the meantime, some jester made me jump out of my skin by making cannon-like explosions. Afterwards, I felt the huge, raised red wheals across Mustafa's neck and arms, but nowhere was the skin broken.

Back to Abéné, where I continued to wait for my genie.

"The *marabout* now has to spend a month in a trance," said Khady.

The rainy season is cutting season in this region. The *kankurangs* were out in force, terrorising people and disrupting their work, as young boys and girls are circumcised. The *kankurang* is common among the Mandinka tribes, the largest ethnic group in The Gambia, and very common in Abéné and northern Casamance. It originated from the *komo*, a secret society of hunters, whose organisation and traditions contributed to the emergence of the Manding. Between around 1230 and 1600, the Mandinka empire, also referred to as the Mali empire, was the largest in West Africa, and it has profoundly influenced the culture of the region, which spreads from what is now northern Guinea through to southern Mali.

Looking like a scary brown monster that clangs two machetes, the *kankurang* wears the bark and red fibre of the *faara* tree. We have one of these trees, and Khady hacked off a bit of bark to demonstrate it to me. This is now tied to Kermit's rear-view mirror. Who needs furry dice?

The *kankurang*'s main purpose appears to be associated with Mandinka circumcision ceremonies. Most boys are circumcised by the time they are 15, and it is believed they are highly susceptible to evil spirits and witches during this time, so the *kankurang* protects them.

The *kankurang* ensures order and justice, as well as the exorcism of evil spirits. He's there to ensure that the complex knowledge and practices underpinning Manding identity are taught. The male initiates must learn about the medicinal value of plants, hunting techniques and so on, although the practice is decreasing with urbanisation and the cultivation of sacred forests. At this point, the ritual becomes more about entertainment, and is trivialised.

One of the initiates will be delegated to wear the *kankurang* mask by the elders. He will then retreat to the forest with other initiates. The *kankurang* will then undertake vigils and processions throughout the village. All of this generally occurs around August-September. The *kankurang* parades around, surrounded by former initiates and other villagers, who follow his behaviour and perform songs and dances while he wields two machetes and cries out in a high-pitched squeal. If, despite his efforts, a cut child falls ill, a stronger *kankurang*, the *fambondi*, is called via an offering of seven peppers, seven stones and seven kola nuts.

During the day, the *kankurang* is simply a man dressed up, teasing children with his machetes. During the night, he is thought to have real powers, and can fly to the top of trees, duplicate himself and make himself invisible as he attacks witches and evil spirits. Some *kankurangs* are thought to make a woman barren if glimpsed by her.

One *kankurang* even arrived at the Little Baobab. I was watering plants with Fakeba and heard the clanging of two machetes and high-pitched screaming as the devil-like creature prowled on the other side of our fence. Then I heard more screaming as Khady, Gulliver and Yama all ran to barricade themselves into the house, terrified. I hid behind a bush and watched the red hairy creature stalking around the house and banging on the windows.

It was accompanied by several young men, one of whom was Fitty. They were collecting for his young son's circumcision ceremony and the *kankurang* was there to intimidate us into giving something.

Later, I went to meet friends at Gerard's French restaurant. As I arrived, there was a big argument going on and another *kankurang* was skulking around, this one making chicken noises. Gerard was fuming. This *kankurang* had entered his bedroom, struck his Senegalese wife to the floor and proceeded to beat her with the machete. She showed me her bruises and a cut across her leg.

One can only respect traditional culture so far, and I didn't blame them for calling the police. But nothing will be done in all likelihood, as everyone, police included, is scared of the *kankurang*. A succession of village elders and the chief did arrive to try to placate them though.

The next day my Senegalese mechanic's Land Rover windscreen was smashed. Then a teacher was attacked on his way to school, his arm cut by the machete. There was no school for the next few weeks as the teachers protested.

Yet again, I found myself questioning my sanity. Back in Europe we'd left behind these beliefs hundreds of years ago, and here I was bringing up my children in this culture. Was this the price I must pay for our normally idyllic lifestyle?

Khady wanted to attend a lads' circumcision ceremony and I accompanied her, but was warned to be very careful not to point my camera at the *kankurang*, or it would smash it. Hundreds of people gathered in a circle and the young boys arrived to the beat of drumming, then performed dances in the circle's centre, each trying to outdo the last, while the *kankurangs* prowled the outskirts menacingly and I meekly kept my camera hidden away.

It was also the day the girls would be cut. The next day, accompanied by *kankurangs* to keep away prying eyes, they'd all go to wash in the salty sea to help heal the wounds.

There have been many *kankurang* attacks on people locally in recent years, which is something the authorities appear afraid to address. But if it's truly believed that the *kankurang* is providing protection and has magical powers, then how can anyone confront him about any misdemeanours?

It was around this time that Fakeba returned a book about African ceremonies that he'd borrowed from me, remarking that he didn't approve of many of the pictures of naked tribesmen with lip plates, scarification and so on.

"These people have no civilisation; they need to modernise like us," he remarked.

Either materials to reveal a genie are difficult to procure, or serious preparation is required, or someone was having a laugh at my expense...

"You'll never guess what; there's this *toubab* who thinks I can show him a genie – what a mug!"

Several months passed, and I was beginning to give up hope of being shown a genie. Once again, I asked Khady what was happening and she called the *marabout*, returning a while later looking sombre.

"Every night he sat awake summoning the genie, but his

sister, she also needed to see it. He revealed it to her, and she went crazy. Now he's trying to save her. She's just howling to the moon every night, talking gibberish. We can't do this Simon; it's too dangerous."

This is Africa, it's very dark and there are some things that I will never understand.

# JUST MUDDLING ALONG

*A lawyer from London has arrived to stay at our guest house. He's seen our prices and decided to travel in West Africa, so he probably isn't expecting five-star luxury but I occasionally feel a bit self-conscious about what we're offering. I have to remind myself we've built everything from scratch in the bush. And besides, we only charge just over £10 per night, including breakfast. Although simple and rustic, it's clean and comfortable.*

*We have a chicken-and-egg situation. To invest and make our surroundings more luxurious I need money, but to charge more money I need the place to be more luxurious. Slowly, slowly, a piece of furniture here, a new electrical connection there, is the way we're going.*

*So, the lawyer is looking around and I show him his house. It's just a simple mud-brick hut with a straw roof. The walls are plastered with oyster-shell cement.*

*His eyes widen.*

*"You have enough oysters here to build a house from the shells?!"*

*Perhaps I am rich after all.*

We have been receiving plenty of guests and getting great reviews, but profits are modest. I plough everything back into further development, and we have built two more roundhouses as well as a tree-top platform, where I sometimes sleep during the hottest months. Waking to the sun rising over our forest is something else.

Making a living here is not easy. I've discovered it's best to keep trying out new things, and never to rely on just one income source.

Five years ago, when I first arrived in Abéné, I barely saw any motorbikes. To get to Abéné from the main road required waiting hours for a bus, or a long walk. So, for a couple of years, Khady ran a motorcycle taxi business. I bought her a bike, and she rented it out to a local lad to drive as a taxi, giving us a small daily income. It seemed a good idea, but now there are 20 or 30 motorcycle taxis.

Everybody seems to copy any tried and tested idea that will support subsistence living, to the point where there are too many people doing it for anyone to do any more than just about get by. In the same way, as more and more new buildings are put up, so more and more new hardware stores keep opening. There must by now be ten or more in Abéné, all selling exactly the same stuff. There are also at least nine internet cafés – and this is a small village.

For a brief period, Khady ran the Senegambia café, a breakfast bar on the main street of Abéné, which, due to the tastiness of her food, was quite successful. I tried encouraging her to experiment, as everywhere sells exactly the same products, so she humoured me and made delicious fish balls in a sweet, reduced Italian-style tomato sauce. Clearly she does know best, as I was the only one who ate it.

Local tastes are very conservative. It seems that if it ain't got fish and it ain't got rice, they ain't gonna eat it. When I served pizza to Khady's younger brother he spat it out in disgust (and it was a decent pizza). Even melting a little butter over a cob of corn was met with screwed-up faces, for corn is eaten dry here. (Oh, and the corn was delicious, and grown on my compost. As predicted, Fakeba's amounted to nothing.) I'll often make European, Chinese or Indian dishes, which the Senegalese will politely try before going back to their *nyankotan*.

"See, I told you, they'll only eat what they know," Khady remarked, and continued to sell bean, mushy peas, spaghetti and spicy fish-paste baguettes like everyone else.

The dream of success didn't last long though. The moment she started getting customers, the restaurant rent was raised, before she could even start to make any profit.

"Oh Africa; too much jealousy," she groaned. This region suffers hugely from jealousy (or envy), and many tell me it's one of Africa's biggest problems. It rages at the family level, in particular, it seems to me, in polygynous households, and extends out into the villages and communities.

Khady decided to bring the business in-house. I saw advantages to this idea. One of the hardest things for a *toubab* to get his head around in Africa is the lack of privacy and personal space. It's not unusual for someone I barely know to turn up at my house, park themselves in my hammock and then not move for the rest of the day – although I've discovered that my very realistic-looking rubber snake solves this problem.

Khady knows our home is my sanctuary. It's where I escape the madness outside. If I want to socialise beyond my family, which now includes Fakeba, Yama, Myamoona and Jumbo, then I'll go out. I'm not a grumpy sod and of course visitors are welcome, but now and again – not all day every day.

I do occasionally become a grumpy sod when I feel taken advantage of. It's impossible for an African to turn someone away from the rice bowl, and my whingeing that I'm already feeding eight people every day invites comments that I am indeed a grumpy sod. As Khady says, people want to come because it's a nice place and we're nice people, so she struggles to understand my point of view. If I am indeed a good man, why would I want to turn people away?

I'm the stranger here and I have to fit in with local norms to a certain extent. But it's also my house and an Englishman's home, even when it is a bunch of mud huts in the African jungle, is his castle. I'm trying to get the balance right. After all, the friendliness and sense of community is a big part of what I love here. But it sure gets a bit much sometimes.

So, when Khady suggested bringing the breakfast bar in-house and creating a bar-restaurant area, I saw an opportunity to create a space where local people could hang out without invading my more private quarters so freely. Possibly they'd even spend some money and buy something. Then, our house and the majority of our land could be for invited guests and family only. So we went ahead.

Construction of the bar was interesting, in an African sort of way, and I'm now fully aware that even the simplest job will involve either an adventure, or complete and utter confusion. Khady asked my advice and I drew a plan for a barbecue grill, bar and cooking work surfaces, all open-air and beneath a straw roof for shade from the sun. Everyone lives outdoors here and I'm baffled that people build structures with hot zinc roofs and tiny windows when they could be open, airy and cool.

The builder looked at my plan, which I also marked out in the sand to make doubly sure. He claimed to have understood, and started to make the foundations. He was Gambian and spoke English, so there was no language issue.

But then I broke one of my Africa rules: never let tradesmen work in my absence – a rule I can't help but break fairly regularly. I went back 20 minutes later to check up, and he'd dug the foundations for a very large roundhouse. No explanation was offered other than that he had decided it would be better than my plan.

"You can divide the house into four rooms: a bar, a restaurant, a sitting area and a shop." Yes, but that was not really what I had in mind. So we went back to plan A.

While our breakfast bar was under construction, a new potential small business opportunity cropped up. Car maintenance was a big problem in Abéné. There were a couple of decent mechanics, and a bunch of less decent ones, but they mostly operated under mango trees with a couple of spanners. Invariably, you would go, they would look, poke around, stand back and tut. Some things are the same everywhere.

"The rubber is finished."

It's always the rubber.

"So where do I get a new one?"

"Gambia."

And thus followed a trip to The Gambia, where I would get ripped off by the Lebanese car-part traders, or I would give the money to the mechanic and pray that he wasn't ripping me off, knowing he probably was, but at least it was a bit cheaper than if I went myself.

Whether for a tiny part or something serious, there was no car-part dealer in Abéné, or in nearby Kafountine. Even in Ziguinchor I was told to go to The Gambia.

Then, when we got the parts, the mechanic would say, "Simon, we need grease." And I would have to drive a couple of kilometres to one of the ten hardware stores (or walk, if the car was incapacitated, but at least I could now get a motorbike taxi) to buy grease.

"Why aren't you selling and profiting from the grease?" I asked Lamin, my regular mechanic. It was then that he proposed his idea to me.

"I want to open the first car-parts store. The first will be the most powerful. This is a good business; no one else is doing it. All the mechanics waste their time and money going to The Gambia every week."

It was a compelling argument. I'd previously thought about doing this myself, but had figured it would be way too expensive.

"I am friends with a Lebanese car dealer. He will sell to us cheaply. We can make a profit and also charge a little for what people would have spent for their travel. We can start small with some brake pads, rubbers, quality oil – no one else sells it here."

So we went to meet the Lebanese guy, Abdou, and for a modest investment, we have kitted out a shop that Lamin had built next to his workshop. Abdou has known Lamin a long time and trusts him. He adds a small mark-up to make it worth his while and we pay back a small amount monthly as we sell the products. With the profits, we can buy more stock and eventually can also sell parts for motorbikes. Additionally, I can get parts for Kermit much cheaper.

What can possibly go wrong?

Well, probably, plenty, given where we are, and I seriously considered heading off into the bush in search of hornbills to bring some luck for the venture. Perhaps I should have. For, within months, there were several other shops undercutting us with cheap Chinese goods. It's very hard to convince someone with hardly any money to spend more, even if by spending twice as much on an original part you will have something that will last three times as long as the cheap Chinese junk.

Still, I've broken even and, to my astonishment, make a small profit now and again.

Khady is always trying something new. Currently, with her sister, she buys fish at the beach and transports it inland in a large ice-box to sell, for quite good returns. Mind you, it took a year or more to cut through the red tape to be able to do this. The State doesn't make it easy for people to get by.

Despite their vast resources, most African countries are not as productive as they should be because, rather than allow economies to grow and entrepreneurs to flourish, all too often the authorities will take the money for themselves, their family members and ethnic group, stifle industry and trade and impose bewildering amounts of bureaucracy. Unfortunately for most Africans, this suits developed nations, as it's so much easier to do business with a few bribes than it is to do it transparently. The developed nations, corporations and a few lucky Africans win, while the majority of the people lose out.

Meanwhile small-scale entrepreneurs also end up having to support huge families and assorted hangers-on, and are unable to invest any profits to grow their businesses. You have to break out of the system to succeed; hence the popularity of trying to escape to Europe.

Khady keeps trying, though, and I'm always happy to help

her with business ideas if I have the means. She insists on paying me back, as she refuses to accept charity. Her next idea was to be a nightclub promoter.

I had thought the various bars in Abéné ran their own parties, but Khady explained that anyone could hire the bar, organise music and drinks, set an entrance fee and make a profit. As the drinks depot allowed her to take the drinks on sale or return, and the DJ and band agreed to vary their fee depending upon the success, it appeared little could go wrong. But of course, I was forgetting where we are.

The party was all set to go, when there was a death in the village. Out of respect, there could be no parties that night, and even the local *djembe* groups cancelled their daily practice, so Khady rescheduled for the following week.

I helped where I could, but left most of the organising to her. She'd roped in many friends to act as doormen, bar tenders and promoters. I was slightly worried that only a few people would come, no one would have cash for drinks and we'd be left out of pocket, but I needn't have feared.

Parties don't usually get busy till past midnight, but by about ten we had a sizeable crowd. Khady is well-loved and we've put on some popular *djembe* performances at home, so everyone turned out to support her. Some time after midnight, when my friends Wakily performed, the place was heaving, and the audience danced up and around the band as their leader, Saly, whipped them up into a frenzy with his vivid facial expressions.

There was one small problem. Khady called me to explain.

"Simon, do you see the barman?"

We'd hired the bar, which came with a barman. I looked over to see the normally angry-looking Skippy smiling back at me. His smile made me nervous.

"He pushed our drinks to the back of the fridge and placed the bar's own at the front. The owner is now demanding we pay for his drinks and he won't accept to swap them for ours," said Khady.

She later explained that the bar owner had gone to a *marabout* so that she wouldn't find out. It can't have been a particularly effective *marabout*, seeing as she did find out – pretty quickly.

Aside from this, we had fun, and plenty of our friends were there, dancing to the *mbalax* rhythms and Nigerian auto-tuned chart hits. My Western music-loving friend Papis saw my dismay at the pop music (although I have been known to shake a leg to "Chop my money") and made a suggestion: "Ask the DJ for Mr Zimmerman."

Being a rock nerd, I understood, but this was an obscure reference to hear in Abéné. Robert Zimmerman usually goes by the name Bob Dylan. Needless to say, there was no Dylan on the playlist.

The next morning, when I came to, I saw Khady arguing with someone in the *bantaba*.

As I approached, Skippy got up and walked off, muttering something about *toubabs* and slavery, which puzzled me as it had been Khady's night and nothing to do with me. Occasionally I come across someone who doesn't like me just because I am white. Khady tells me this is usually because they're angry about slavery. I'd just woken up and wanted a coffee, not a debate about this slightly contentious reading of history.

While Europeans certainly industrialised the slave trade, it was a trade that had already been present for millennia, and indeed it still occurs. Muslims took white slaves during the Barbary wars of the early 1800s; there are currently thought to be 100,000 slaves in Mauritania; rebels are enslaving women in Nigeria and elsewhere in the Sahel, and domestic servitude is still common in Senegal. The issues involved are usually immensely complex, rarely black and white, and quite frankly I'm tired of the lazy thinking that puts all the blame on me, so I went off and made my coffee.

"Forget him," said Khady. "He's just angry that he couldn't cheat us, but it's sorted now." After all the costs were paid, Khady made a healthy profit of more than £100, which is a huge amount in Abéné.

I'm getting an inkling of how Basil Fawlty must feel as I run around trying to keep our guest house business ticking over. It's one thing trying to organise your house in Africa when you are simply getting on with life, but quite another when you have paying guests. At least in the UK, you have a choice of wholesalers selling individual packets of cornflakes and all the supplies you need. If something is missing you can nip to the corner shop. It's very different here.

One day I received a call mid-morning from 20 guests who wanted to come for dinner that evening, and stipulating that they also required a healthy supply of ice-cold beer. The nearest supermarkets are about 60 kilometres and a border crossing away, and it's not always guaranteed that the local shops carry stock, but we managed.

Another time, I promised guests a *koumpo* dance and drum lessons – and then spent five days getting no response from either dancers or drummers. Although *koumpo* dancers are forest spirits, they do use a mobile phone, but as they live deep in the forest they don't always have a good signal.

It all worked out – it always does – but like any project, it got a little stressful. I'd organised transport for the 40 or 50 *koumpo* dancers, but the driver called shortly before the agreed time to say that his vehicle had broken down. Somehow we found a replacement. Then a rival guest house owner spotted my guests arriving in the village and tried to take them to his own camp, telling them it was mine. Confusingly, he has named his place "Les Baobabs," so now I need to ensure future guests reach the real "Little Baobab."

I'm very proud of my team, who work really hard to give our guests a special experience. They have sometimes unfathomable notions of Western standards, timekeeping and environmental responsibility, but they mean well and do a great job.

They say that if you start a business in a recession and it survives, then you'll be fine; it's only ever going to get easier. Despite plenty of empty guest houses lying around the region, I hoped I'd have a fair chance of capturing the Anglophone market, especially as I'd started building a web following through my website and articles and my first book. Not to mention having chased several hornbills, buried countless goat's horns and possessing enough *gris-gris* to make me invincible. What I hadn't counted on was the double whammy inflicted upon the Senegalese tourist industry over the past few years.

First, a visa was introduced, right around the time we opened for business. Instead of simply turning up at the border or airport and gaining a two-month entry stamp, tourists had to apply online or in an embassy, through a convoluted process that many gave up on, and then cough up 50 euros per person. The figure I heard quoted several times was that tourist numbers dropped to less than a third of usual levels. It was by all accounts Youssou N'Dour, the then tourism minister, who'd introduced the visa. This is the guy who'd probably done more than anyone in the country to bring tourists to Senegal and raise awareness of African music in the late Eighties and early Nineties, and yet, here he was now, making it harder for folk to visit.

Many Senegalese I discussed this with felt a visa to be a positive move. Why should we Europeans just waltz in, when the Senegalese have to jump through hoops to travel to the West? I agree that this isn't fair, but then again, the vast majority of Europeans visiting Senegal are bringing significant tourist income or settling, like me, starting businesses, paying into the local economy and providing employment.

Since I've been living here, countless young men I've known have hooked up with a much older European woman, gained their papers (for which she would have paid) and then done a runner upon arrival in Europe. Along with the illegal immigration of West Africans via Libya, it's not too surprising that Europe is battening down the hatches, although this isn't much consolation for those genuinely escaping war zones, or people like Khady who just want to go for a short visit. My tentative enquiries about acquiring a visa for Khady reveal that it's likely to be a long, difficult and expensive process, even for just the tourist visa we need so she can accompany the kids to see their grandparents.

Then, not long after the visa was introduced and tourist regions started feeling the pinch, Ebola struck Sierra Leone, Liberia and Guinea to the south, proving my point about the importance of multiple income streams. Many tourists cancelled holidays here and elsewhere in West Africa to avoid the risk. The Gambia, which relies on tourism, even suffered from food shortages in the eastern regions. There's probably barely a family in that country that doesn't have one or more members working in the hotels or restaurants of the Smiling Coast, so when hotel occupancy dipped to 30% and staff were laid off, the entire country felt the pain.

One outcome of the Ebola crisis was that it gave the Senegalese government an excuse to withdraw the visa without losing face, as one of a number of measures to attract tourists. Eighteen months after it was introduced, it was quietly dropped. And, thankfully, Ebola now appears to be under control, with no further cases in Senegal.

"Khady's Jungle Bar and Grill" eventually opened to great fanfare with many guests, a drum troupe and a disco, and pizzas made by me.

A surprise guest was Skippy, who started to turn up for the occasional *pastis*, the French Pernod-like liqueur popular here. Although most Muslims in Abéné don't drink alcohol, quite a few of the young guys do, especially when they are somewhere off the beaten track where others won't see them.

"I expect Allah knows you're drinking," I said grumpily, as I didn't like the guy.

"But I'm not a Muslim and I'm not a Christian," he replied.

I was surprised, as it's rare to meet someone who's not religious. I probed further.

"I'm a Bassari, from the east of the country. I'm an animist, I worship the nature spirits."

He was clearly very proud of the fact and he told me more about his tribe and homelands.

"But it's not enough to talk about the Bassari, you must come and see for yourself. We have an initiation ceremony soon."

It was a warm and generous offer, and slowly I began warming to the man. I'm invited to so many ceremonies that I wouldn't have a lot of time to live my own life if I were to attend each and every one, but this one would be something else. I'd read and heard about the Bassari, with their distinctive traditions and masks, so I vowed to myself that I'd go.

Later that evening, sitting behind the bar chatting to a guest, I sighed wearily and raised my beer to my lips, saying something about hoping I might one day be able to relax a bit.

The look on her face said it all. Here I was, in a small jungle clearing in a bar that I own, with guaranteed sunshine and a steady stream of lovely people, with whom I spend my days chatting and socialising and sharing my passions for Africa, travel and adventure.

I may be only just muddling along, but I'm not exactly working down a pit.

# THE WILD EAST

*"Boom!!! Although I'm well used to it by now, I still jump out of my skin each time the bomb goes off, which is about every five minutes. Skippy and some other guys are stuffing a mixture of gunpowder and couscous powder into a metal tube, setting a fuse, running for safety and watching the crowds freak out.*

*In front of me an initiate stands staring impassively while an older man holds a chicken by its legs and swings the fowl around the younger guy's head. Then the chicken is stretched out and its head chopped off.*

*The headless chicken falls to the ground and runs in circles – I swear it is still clucking – while the initiate chases it, still looking emotionless. He catches up and the chicken quivers to a halt as the boy beats it with the stick.*

*Afterwards, the older man examines the testicles – the chicken's, not the initiate's. White is a good omen and black bad. I later hear a rumour the initiate will be ritually sacrificed if they are black, but on this occasion they're white.*

*We all breathe a sigh of relief as the chicken joins others already hung in the trees like a macabre art installation.*

The temperatures and humidity were beginning to rise and the rains were imminent when I received a message from Skippy, telling me the initiation ceremonies of his mysterious Bassari tribe would begin the following week. He was there and I should head over to meet him. Visiting the Bassari lands with a local was an opportunity I couldn't afford to miss.

I travelled by *sept places* bush taxis – the ubiquitous Peugeot station wagons, 504s and 505s, all 20 to 40 years old and probably going way beyond what their French manufacturers ever expected. They're high sprung at the back, and possibly jacked up even further to negotiate the potholes of West Africa. They are also fitted with a third row of seats where the boot would normally be. Although in Senegal they're restricted to eight people (one driver and seven passengers), not including babies and young children, in the east of Senegal and parts of Guinea they carry nine passengers.

By the afternoon of the first day, the air blowing into the bush taxi felt like a hairdryer with the heat turned up to the max. I wondered, not for the first time, why it is that I emerge looking like a sweating stumbling zombie covered in grime, while the girl next to me looks cool and calm in her pure white dress?

When I reached the hotel in Tambacounda, the thermometer read a cool 40°C, which was far more pleasant than the last time I visited. On that occasion, it was closer to 50°C, with near 100% humidity. Tamba is a pretty groovy place, though, and I found a half-decent hotel, which even had a pool, although it was positioned near a mosque, which I wouldn't recommend if you enjoy a lie-in. After a dip, I felt semi-human again, and then found a chop shop selling pizzas to take away. Tamba was doing me proud. The tomato sauce was ketchup-based, but hey, I'm several hundred kilometres into the middle of nowhere in the dusty Sahel, not in Napoli.

I found a bar for a luke-cold beer, but the table I placed it on may as well have been a hot plate. When the power wasn't out, the television was showing a Brazilian soap opera, which, to my eyes, boasted far better acting and production values than the popular Argentinian ones. Then there was a Senegalese chat show, where the guests wore shades in a dark studio. The sun never sets in the land of the cool.

The next day I arrived at the *gare routière*, found a bush taxi, jumped in and headed to Niokolokoba, a national park the size of Wales. Well, that's what I've read somewhere. I've not checked its exact area, but anywhere that is quite big is typically described as being the size of Wales. I believe this is one of the rules of travel writing.

I stayed a night at Wassadou lodge, positioned high on the banks of a bend in the river Gambia at the edge of Niokolokoba national park. It didn't take me long to dump my belongings and perch myself on a comfy chair overlooking the river, with a suitably cold, hop-based beverage in hand as the sun set.

A crocodile slipped into the water from a sandbank. Then

a gazelle sauntered down for a drink. I was hoping the croc had its eye on the ball, and sat with the camera ready, but it seemed it wasn't hungry. Then I spotted a couple of hippos. I'm always tempted to go and swim with them but the reality is they're one of the deadliest of all African mammals, and although I like to think that I'm a swashbuckler, I'd rather not go down in history as a viral Youtube clip.

Still, I took a boat trip. I saw another hippo, and the boatman cautiously approached. We were at quite a distance, but this hippo was an angry one. He spluttered water through his nose then disappeared, leaving a whirlpool of bubbles, before launching himself out of the water about ten metres away and hurtling towards us. The boatman speedily motored us to safety and I returned to the lodge, exhilarated and thirsty.

At a mere 38°C, Kedegou, the main administrative centre of south-east Senegal, seemed cooler, although sitting under a tin roof waiting for a mini-bus to fill for three hours felt very much like sitting in an oven.

As always with these forms of transport, there were a few false starts. First for fuel and tyre-pressure checks. Then to load more gear. Then a mysterious stop where everyone argued and got a little boisterous but nothing much seemed to happen.

I sat sweating while locals took it all in their stride, seemingly cool as cucumbers. The minibus was very similar to the one that I had crashed in four years previously and I was sitting in the same seat – the so-called death seat, up next to the driver. I'd only just about recovered the nerve to travel in these battered old death traps, and I must admit I was scared a few times on this journey, one notable instance being when it hurtled down a hill, skidded around a sharp bend sending dust everywhere, and narrowly missed a herd of cows.

The sun was going down as I reached Salamata, a Fula village tucked into the base of the so-called mountains. The highest is only 300 metres or so. Skippy had reserved rooms at the Camar Inn, and was waiting for me at this friendly and very rustic (travellers' speak for basic) lodge, which thankfully had a fridge, and rustled up some fish and rice. The room was decent enough but had no windows, so I spent the night lying there feeling as if I was being crawled over by ants as the sweat dripped ticklishly.

The next day Skippy and I set off to walk across the "mountain range" to Ethiolo, the Bassari village. He'd rustled up a pick-up truck that took us part of the way, up a deeply rutted track, then we walked across very dry grass slopes, passing shea butter trees on the branches of which, we saw some chameleons. No doubt they were much relieved that our maleness would mean they could remain un-doused by shots of milk.

As we walked, Skippy told me his story, which perhaps goes some way to explaining why he'd struck me as so angry when I first met him. Had I been through what he had, I'm sure I'd be mad at the world. He turned out to be very sweet and vulnerable, and when I thought back to how intimidated he made me feel the first time I met him, it just goes to show how wrong first impressions can be.

Although he spoke English with a Gambian accent, he'd only been there for a couple of years, hustling mainly in the tourist resorts.

"I had many *toubab* friends and many girlfriends. I'd take one to the airport, declare my love, and half an hour later the next would be arriving." Knowing the guys in these parts, I wasn't massively surprised.

Before The Gambia, he'd travelled around West Africa buying masks and artefacts, which he'd sell to the tourist boutiques in Dakar, Bamako or Banjul.

"I spent some time in Nigeria and met a girl there; we had a baby." I could see pain in his eyes and he turned away, looking as if he was holding back tears.

"It's okay, you don't have to tell me."

"No, no, it's fine. It makes me feel better if I share the story. It feels like a dream now, but the girl, my *chérie*, she went mad. I had to leave her there."

Skippy launched into the story and I had the growing sensation of feeling as if I were in a horror film. His girl had been travelling by bus in a big city, having just shopped at the market. In the packed bus, a razor blade-wielding thief had attempted to slash the bag slung over her shoulder. Except that he had made a mistake.

"Simon, she felt something warm dripping onto her foot, and at the same time our baby started screaming."

"She loved that child more than anything." Tears were streaming down Skippy's face by now and I urged him to stop, but on he went, not saying explicitly what had happened to the baby. But the pain in his eyes told me enough.

"The African mob will have its own justice. This is Africa; it's very dark here. She knew that, and she wanted him to suffer. If the people saw what had happened, they'd kill him immediately. She took his wrist, and he must have realised what he'd done because he didn't resist. He knew he couldn't, or else he'd be killed. She had a needle for fixing her hair in her purse. She pushed its point under the nail of his finger and plunged it deep. He knew he couldn't scream and she told me everything. About how his sweat started pouring, how he breathed so heavily, how he was choking back the puke, how he was shaking uncontrollably. She did three nails before the other passengers noticed. The last she saw of him was as he was swallowed up by the crowd and his arm was ripped off at the shoulder."

I sometimes get frustrated about media perceptions of Africa and the way they focus on a never-ending spiral of misery, corruption, war, poverty, famine, primitive surroundings and disease. There are plenty of feel-good success stories here that are ignored, but then I hear stories like this, and I have to accept that it can indeed be extreme at times.

We stopped at a Bassari compound of simple round huts made from lumps of deep red laterite rock, constructed like an English drystone wall and thatched with grass. Lined up outside were some long bows. A grandma came out and offered us a dirty plastic cup of delicious millet beer. Before long we'd arrived in Ethiolo. It was about 11am and the sun was brutal. Standing outside on the iron-rich gravel, I could feel the heat reflecting up at me. I was afraid I might melt.

The main camp in town was fully booked but I was told I could sleep on a mat on the floor of the restaurant. The camp was run by the charismatic Balingho, a very welcoming old Bassari man who infused the surrounding atmosphere with the reek of palm wine whenever he was around.

I was invited to drink *attaya* tea with some people who turned out to be the village teachers. Mr Diallo and Mr Ba were from Dakar, and had been posted here by the government. To me, passing through for a few days, it felt like heaven. They weren't so convinced.

"I've been here three years. There's no electricity, no fridge, no nothing. The only thing to enjoy is palm wine, but I'm Muslim and I can't drink it," said Mr Ba, looking downcast.

Balingho explained the complicated initiation ceremony, where initiates pass through a series of huts at different ages, and are beaten if they fail to attend, or to attain new levels of maturity. After the ceremonies in the hut, the boys dance from village to village for seven days before going to live in a cave. Skippy helped translate some of the trickier bits, dropping into the conversation that he himself would need to be beaten twice next year as part of his own initiation process.

"Does it hurt?" I asked, wondering if it was symbolic. He laughed nervously and said yes.

We sat listlessly until 3pm – the beginning of the end of the hot bit and almost the start of the slightly less hot bit of the day. Then we set off up the hill to check out the Koré ceremony, in which the initiated boys march back from months spent living in caves in the surrounding forests and hills to undertake the chicken test and then fight.

The Bassari are a small tribe that lives as hunters and farmers in the rocky escarpments and foothills of the Fouta Djalon, which spreads out from south-east Senegal into Guinea. Skippy explained that in Bassari society, roles and responsibilities are defined by a person's place in a very strict chronological hierarchy, far more so than most traditional societies. Order is enforced by the older level.

There are seven stages for men, and Koré is the most important ceremony, marking the passage into adulthood. The boys are separated from their families and live in communal houses for several months, away from females.

For the initiation, older initiates take them to the sacred forest where legend states the boys are killed and eaten by Numba, a chameleon deity, who then regurgitates them as young adults. Had I ended up staying here instead of Abéné, who knows, perhaps my first book could have been "Regurgitated by chameleons."

Before they enter the forest, they are washed and rubbed with palm oil by older women who then braid their hair and tie in feathers from sacrificed chickens. They endure a series of harsh rituals and emerge from the forest acting like infants. Their guardians, older initiates, must wash, feed and even put them to sleep. From this state of regression, they emerge as mature adults. I later discovered that throughout the ritual, boys must not smile, laugh, talk or even look from side to side, or else they'll be severely punished. Which explains why they did indeed look so passive.

Several local-style huts – the initiation huts – sat around a clearing among some large trees. The entire area was bustling with activity: ladies selling drinks (one superstar had dragged ice up to this outpost), snacks, goats and some tack. Cauldrons bubbled on fires and many people gathered to socialise. Young men who were being initiated wore their hair plaited and, for reasons unknown to me, football outfits. Tradition and modernity side by side. There were some delicious local drinks available and I made it my business to try them. The palm wine was fantastically rich, tasting to me as if honey had been added, though apparently this was not the case. Then there was an actual honey wine, which was sublime.

Youngsters were constantly blowing whistles. This cacophony gradually intensified, some chanting was heard and then a procession of young men arrived down a slope to circle around the ceremonial area, shuffling along as someone played a local flute.

A couple of cows and many goats were slaughtered before us as well. The dead cows were hung in a tree.

As darkness fell, I was invited to eat *foufou*, a tasteless manioc paste smothered with a tasteless manioc leaf sauce. This functions more as a gut filler than as something to savour.

Later, Skippy appeared with a beautiful girl who can't have been much more than 20 years in age. He had a proposition.

"This is my sister; please sleep with her." As with "brother", the term "sister" rarely means an actual sibling. Whatever, she looked game and not under any pressure, but my Western morals kicked in.

"Skippy, she looks gorgeous, but you know I have Khady and the kids."

"But they're in Abéné and you are here. We are all men..."

All the while, the dancers trooped around chanting, like a tribal conga. It was fantastic. Fires lit up the area, and dancers congaed at least until midnight, in an increasingly inebriated atmosphere.

Eventually, in the small hours, I headed back to the camp. When I was about halfway there, the heavens opened: my first rain in around eight months. It was cool and pleasant – until the ground turned into a quagmire and my flip-flops got stuck and broke. I entered the restaurant area where I'd spread out my straw mat only to find it taken. I was exhausted, and simply pulled off my soaking wet T-shirt, placed it on the gravel floor and lay down on top of it.

A Senegalese guy woke up and invited me to lie on his mat, which I did.

"Where are you sleeping?" I asked.

"With you," he replied. As my bag had been locked in somebody's room for safety, I had nothing except the drenched clothes I was wearing, so I lay in my wet shorts on the hard straw mat next to the large Senegalese chap and promptly fell asleep. About 2am, I woke, cold, damp and under attack from ants, and that was the end of my sleep. Oh, what a night.

Balingho came round and made us get up at 6am to set the table for breakfast. I couldn't face the dry bread and margarine, so after a few coffees, Skippy and I walked back up the hill for the main event of the Koré, something I'd seen previously in photographs and was eagerly awaiting.

A procession of dancers snaked slowly down the mountain wearing their distinctive cartwheel masks. They represent nature, and oversee the festivities, ensuring traditions are maintained. Their bodies were painted with ochre and their faces hidden by gauze. I could hear whistles, chanting and screams as they appeared at the top of the ridge across a valley. Slowly, they wound their way down the track, mimicking the movements of a chameleon. They are said to have the power of the sacred chameleon, and their presence at a ceremony is considered very auspicious.

As they approached, I moved up the slope, trying to get out of the way, but at the last moment they turned and came towards me, passing within inches. At the head of the procession was a masked creature with a ring of leaves tied around its chest, similar to the Diola *Essamaye* mask. Still they came, perhaps 50 masked dancers. Shortly after they'd passed me they whooped and started running down the mountain as Skippy, myself and other villagers tried to keep up without stumbling.

The next phase of the ceremony was forbidden to females and cameras – something that nobody had told us beforehand. One *toubab* went to take a shot and was whacked soundly with a stick.

A little way down the mountain was a large open space around which the audience formed a circle. The masked dancers removed their cartwheel masks but continued to wear the bark hoods and visors as they formed a line along one edge of the circle. As with many African events, there were too many Indians and not enough Chiefs. Everyone was shouting orders, and chaos ensued, but eventually, the next phase began: *lutte*; traditional Senegalese wrestling.

The young initiates took turns to fight the older and much bigger, hooded creatures as a measure of their courage and virility. The small boys, some looking about 13 years old, approached the giants, holding heavy sticks and shields. I could hear the thud of wood on flesh before they locked bodies and wrestled in the more traditional sense. It's not necessary for the initiate to win, as long as he fights like a man. Following this, he receives a new name and status before being presented back to his parents as a stranger with a similar appearance to the boy who'd left months earlier.

Most of the initiates were beaten, but eventually one little Scrappy Doo-like character went in quickly and knocked his opponent off-balance, landing him on his back. The arena exploded, with everyone dancing into the circle and whooping for joy as the initiate was carried away on the shoulders of other boys.

We returned to the initiation area on the side of the mountain as those home-made cannons boomed, then chickens were slaughtered, initiates chased after them and testicles were inspected. The snake-like conga, the chanting and dancing continued well into the night, as it had done every year since anyone could remember. As I drank palm wine, chatted to villagers and occasionally joined the conga, I ruminated on the fact that the intense heat and the arduous travel had been a small price to pay for the chance to experience such an otherworldly, timeless ceremony.

# OFFICIAL INSANITY

*Fitty Futta turns up, looking every bit the "Del boy" in his new Burberry flat cap.*

*"Of course I can arrange your driving licence; yes-aye."*

*It isn't strictly necessary for me to be present for an eye test or a medical. However, I will have to undertake a theory test.*

*"Wait, wait. A theory test? In French?"*

*"No problem. Don't worry; be happy. I'll pay them; you'll pass. Just show your face; yes-aye".*

*I'm told to wait in a dank corridor with 30 others. Rather worryingly, they are all clutching and reading the local Highway Code book. Fitty has disappeared and I don't know what's going on. Even if I have already passed, I don't want to make a tit of myself.*

*We are led into a room where they call a register. There is a large chart with road signs. Pointing at one of these, the examiner makes every single person say what it means. Of course, once the first person has spoken, everyone else just copies. Except for me. I am about to repeat the French when the examiner says, "In English, please".*

*It's a red triangle, blank white inside. I don't recall ever having seen a road sign in Senegal, and certainly not this one, so I am forced to guess – incorrectly, as it transpires.*

*The second symbol is a blue triangle with 30 written inside it. I say it's a speed limit (though I've no idea why it's blue). Wrong. Then I get the third one wrong. That's it; the test is over, and we all troop out.*

*Later, Fitty reappears, congratulates me and tells me I've passed.*

*"Yes-aye!"*

*Now I just have to return in a month to do my practical test.*

Some years ago, I found myself wondering why so many young, talented people in countries such as Senegal emigrate rather than staying to help develop their homelands. I'm no longer surprised. Now I have seen at first hand how the local officials treat their people. I can see also how patriotism is easily lost.

It is a shame. Africa needs its young people – especially the skilled ones – to remain *in situ* and help it to develop. I encounter way too much intelligence and resourcefulness here to believe that the problem with Africa is Africans themselves – a view I have often heard. I would say it's the general lack of education and the economic and political environment that make it so difficult for individuals to excel.

The result is that much of Africa's talent, rather than being productive is wasting most of its energy in trying to work within this flawed system. What might appear counter-productive and venal is simply necessary for survival. When Africans have an environment in which they can put their intelligence to work more productively, then I'm pretty sure there will be an explosion of economic activity.

Occasionally I meet eloquent young people determined to build their business or do something useful. They are the heroes, refusing to be broken by regimes, by corruption, by bureaucratic nonsense, and I hope their optimism is not crushed out of them.

In the 1600s, West Africa was richer than Europe, whereas now, some areas are arguably worse off than when contact was first made with Europeans. In recent years, the West has raced ahead with its technology. As a result, life has changed dramatically, often without there being any time to consider whether that change is really so desirable. Meanwhile, here in Senegal, life is in many ways pretty much the same as it was hundreds of years ago.

It's amazing how quickly we get used to our technologies and take them for granted. When I'm grumbling about the lack of internet, or indeed, power, it's easy to forget that basic electricity was only introduced to Abéné a decade or so ago.

Every time I wander along to the internet café in Abéné, I take the risk that there will be either no connection or no current. I guess one or other of these problems occurs about 50% of the times I go there. In the UK I'll get frustrated if a webpage takes more than a few seconds to load, whereas here I'm wearily resigned to waiting five minutes or more to download each email.

Together, this inefficiency of technology and the at times inappropriate efficiency or otherwise of African bureaucracy and officialdom can pack a pretty heavy punch. Once, after about two weeks sans internet connection in Abéné, I got so frustrated that I drove all the way to The Gambia in order to get some work done. I'm slightly envious of the many *toubabs* here who shun social media and regular connections; my tourist business relies on emailing guests and posting blog updates, and besides, I love keeping up to date with friends around the world.

I left for The Gambia in the morning after the first heavy rains, taking the back route again. There was another of the regular petty trade disputes going on between The Gambia and Senegal, so there was no guarantee I'd be able to cross over at the official border. Despite The Gambia being populated by the same tribes as the surrounding provinces of Senegal, sharing the same languages, cultures and geography, and with most families being split between the two countries, which were the artificial creations of the British and the French, the border is often closed to vehicles. It was for the first four months of 2016, massively impacting local traders and those transporting goods from Dakar to the Casamance.

Ironically, it seems to me, this is due to petty trade disputes between two nations, both so proud to have thrown off their colonial shackles, yet now fighting across the self-same arbitrary lines originally drawn on maps by those ruling colonial powers. Often forcing warring tribes into one nation, these arbitrarily created national borders could hardly give the newly independent countries a flying start, and have certainly played a role in hindering their development.

Having wrongly presumed that the first rains would quickly drain away, I once again found myself with water washing across Kermit's bonnet. In one village, a guy flagged me down, asking if I could give him a lift.

"No problem."

Immediately, about 15 women appeared from behind some bushes, all loaded up with baskets. They jumped in the back and, yes, I should have said no to some of them, but I decided that on these back roads it probably wouldn't be a big problem. This village was a former rebel stronghold, so it was good for my reputation to help the people there.

Off we went, looking like the hillbilly gang. At a checkpoint on the border, I was reprimanded by the military for overloading, which is a joke when you see how local vehicles transport goods. I pleaded for half an hour and was eventually waved on, without paying a bribe, although the embarrassed villagers had slipped me some cash to help me do so. Instead, I put it towards fuel.

Shortly afterwards, I reached the military checkpoint at the Gambian frontier. A couple of guys with AK-47s sat under a palm-leaf shack. It was in the middle of nowhere – just them, plenty of mud and some bird noises. We stopped and got out and they informed me I'd parked in the wrong place. I had to move back two or three metres to a slightly different patch of completely empty track. Still, I smiled, and greeted them in

Diola, which didn't quite manage to raise a smile from them, but they waved us on.

I jumped back into Kermit and, as it was a dirt track, where the going is slow, I neglected to put on my seat belt. There was a piercing whistle as I passed a hidden police checkpoint, and there ensued a 30-minute "discussion" in which Sherif the policeman assured me this was nothing to do with me being a *toubab* and he dearly wanted to be my friend, but I'd broken the law, and he had no choice but to fine me.

"But good friends don't fine each other," I argued.

"Oh, if it was only that simple," Sherif replied wearily, before spouting ten minutes of cod philosophy and some hard-luck story about how he had to pay his colleagues for my mistakes, even though he was there alone. I eventually got away with paying about £1.50 and vowing not to be so stupid again. We've since become Facebook friends and every time I return on this route he greets me as if we are indeed best friends.

I also made friends with an immigration officer at Gambian customs a few months ago, who asked if he could visit me. They all ask that, so I said "sure", and thought no more of it, but this guy actually came and drank coffee with me at the Little Baobab. This was not a bad thing, as I've been able to sail through immigration ever since, and I can always call him if I have any problems. Most recently, he greeted me with a hug, inquiring after my sons, and I then asked him about his seven sons – he's younger than I am.

Anyway, when I finally reached the internet café in The

Gambia that morning, I was greeted with those dreaded words: "The power is offed."

There's nothing like officialdom and bureaucracy for making me lose my cool. Most other things only get as far as making me feel mildly irritated, but red tape and official obstacles are something else.

Which is why it always helps to know a man. A man who can.

At one point, I opened a bank account in The Gambia, for which I had been promised monthly bank statements by email as well as access to internet banking, neither of which had materialised a year later, despite my regular requests.

My friends knew a senior manager, Sheik Yerbati (pronounced "Shake Your Booty"), so they introduced me to him. He gave the order to a bank clerk and I'd barely shaken my booty before I had been connected.

While discussing life in Senegal, Mr Booty told me he could never live in a Francophone African country, as everything takes forever and, given the option of making something complicated or simple, they'll always choose the former. He's got at least a partial point. It may specialise in blocking the way with checkpoints every ten miles (it definitely does), but, apart from the unaccountable delays at Mr Booty's bank, The Gambia tends to be relatively straightforward when it comes to paperwork.

For example, to get a driving licence, you just buy one or

two relevant documents, take them to an office with a photo and some more cash, and they give you at least temporary papers on the spot. I don't recall their even asking to look at my British driving licence.

But I only discovered this after a long and ultimately fruitless quest to get one in Senegal, where it's a very different matter...

I've held a British driving licence for more than 25 years, which I had always shown at police checkpoints, but one day they told me I needed a local one. I prefer to dot my 'i's and cross my 't's when it comes to paperwork; otherwise I know I'll end up paying bribes. So I set about trying to get a Senegalese driving licence.

This involved at least four trips to Ziguinchor. Once I'd found the licensing office, I was given a long list of requirements. They told me it wasn't a simple matter of checking my licence and issuing a local one. Again, I needed a fixer, and Khady knew just the person.

Fitty Futta certainly seemed very knowledgeable about what needed to be done. He explained the lengthy, convoluted process and we agreed a price, much of which was to buy the various papers I needed. And, of course, to ensure that I 'passed' all the necessary tests, whether or not I actually performed satisfactorily in them, which would involve Fitty in some behind-the-scenes financial transactions, it seemed. Given that I'm a better driver than almost anyone on the road, and hold a good, clean British licence, I didn't feel any guilt about this.

The first of these tests was the interesting ritual described above. The second was no less bewildering.

A month after the theory test, on a dreary December morning, I was back in Ziguinchor once more for my practical test. Apparently I just had to drive to the end of the street and back. I should be able to manage that, but even if I didn't, I'd already passed. Or so I believed.

Not so fast, *toubab*. I found myself outside a large, decaying, colonial French building, with wooden slatted shutters, tired yellow-ochre paint and black damp marks creeping up the walls. Under a large banyan tree stood about 200 men, all waiting as a bloke at the front shuffled through papers and called out names.

"Lamin Diabang, Yayha Deidou, Mohammed Diatta, Semen Feenson…"

I stood by the crowd of young men, wondering what the hell was going on. It seemed to be barely organised chaos but, one by one, we were called forward to perform a three-point turn in front of everyone else. Some people received a cheer and others not. I couldn't work out why, as they all seemed to be doing the same thing.

Finally, I was called. I was feeling the pressure of several hundred people watching the only *toubab*'s every move. It's just a formality, I thought, executed a perfect three-point turn and got out of the car, expecting a cheer.

"Bad luck," said one guy as I returned to the throng.

It appeared I hadn't indicated when I was reversing. I was unaware one should indicate while making a three-point turn, so I guess it's a French thing.

Senegal is a serious country. Officials tend to abide by the rules and, as a *toubab*, it's hard to bend them like the locals do, unless, of course, you know a man. In theory, this is fine by me, as I don't like bowing to corruption. The inherent corruption of public institutions such as the police, the civil service and the law is a major bar to development and progress here.

In practice, however, the downside of my high-minded morals is that I can't get anything done. More than one year after the driving tests, I still hadn't received the licence, Fitty was no longer taking my calls, and I still wasn't 100% sure whether I'd passed or not.

Omar the driver then told me that there was an official Senegalese policy for *toubabs* not to be issued with driving licences. This was due to the fact that a Senegalese licence was valid in France, so French drivers who'd been banned in France were buying licences in Senegal. Rather than investigate any French drivers, they simply stopped giving out licences to all *toubabs*. They still took my money, though.

It's not just *toubabs* like myself who struggle. Khady's identity card took a couple of years. This in spite of being a Senegalese citizen with a birth certificate and a valid claim.

It eventually transpired that everything I'd gone through to get the licence was for nought. A Senegalese driving licence would have been a useless piece of paper for me, anyway; with a Gambian-plated car, I actually needed a Gambian licence. But I found this out the hard way, too...

I'd bought Kermit in The Gambia, and retained his Gambian licence plates, because cars more than eight years old cannot be licenced in Senegal. This is supposedly about keeping old cars off the road, although when you see what's already on the road, it doesn't make a lot of sense. A more plausible explanation is that Karim Wade, the ex-president's son, used to run the local car factory and he didn't want competition. Consequently, all the old cars go straight to The Gambia, which has a thriving secondhand car market.

After the commencement of Macky Sall's new government, this younger Wade was sentenced to jail for six years on corruption charges, although he was soon pardoned and released, due to pressure from religious leaders, and is tipped as a future president. Plus ça change...

Because of this odd law, many drivers near the border buy cheaper Gambian vehicles. And customs had been tightening up the rules – as I found out when I tried to enter Senegal from neighbouring Guinea Bissau.

I had taken some guests on a drive down to the capital of Guinea, which, quite frankly, wasn't one of my better ideas, as we spent the entire trip negotiating with traffic cops, customs men and soldiers. As we approached the frontier to return to Senegal, I assured them that all would be okay from now on. It was early in the morning, we'd cross the border quickly and take a leisurely coffee by the river in Ziguinchor before heading back to the Little Baobab for lunch.

I spoke too soon. The customs guard demanded a Gambian driving licence for my Gambian car, saying that without this we'd be going nowhere. Then, to cap it all, the customs chief helpfully pointed out that if I didn't find a solution soon, he'd impound the car.

Looking on the bright side, that implied there must *be* a solution, so I pleaded with him, but he quickly became annoyed and simply ignored me, as if I were an annoying mosquito he couldn't even be bothered to swat.

"Even if you give one million euros I won't allow you to enter," he eventually muttered, snatching the keys from my hand and retiring to his hammock. From then on, the only response I got was "not my problem" and a flutter of his hand as he didn't even bother to open his eyes.

I was now coordinating the defence with Khady by telephone, and she was discussing the issue with friends and family, some of whom knew customs officials. If I could find a Gambian national with a licence, she told me, then he could drive the car through the frontier for me. Well, where do you find a Gambian on a Sunday afternoon (hours were passing, and all plans to be home for lunch had long since melted away), more than 100 kilometres south of that country, and on the border with another?

Of course, with a few calls here and there, we found someone who knew one. I shelled out for some fixers to travel by public transport to and from Ziguinchor and eventually our saviour arrived. He was a small, elderly man in a *boubou* and skull cap, gripping his prayer beads.

Finally, as darkness fell, we were off. Kind of. He stalled a few times, grated the gears, pulled off too fast, nearly hitting a cyclist, and then off we puttered, like the doddering old driver that he was. But, hey, rather that than someone with 25 years of good driving history but the wrong driving licence. This, after all, is Africa.

Omar the driver later opined that I should just have given the chief some notes, and not even discussed cash. Then, he reckons, we would probably have been back home in time for lunch.

I was recently having a few beers with my *toubab* friends, one of whom was complaining about her adventures in the land of arbitrarily officious officialdom – quite rightly, actually. She'd imported 30 boxes of medical supplies to distribute to local clinics and they had all been confiscated by customs at the Gambia-Senegal border.

"This is for your children, your women, your people," she had told the official.

"But I don't care," he had replied, nonchalantly.

I think that would have tipped me over the edge. Africa is its own worst enemy and such official insanities serve only to hinder its own development. My suggestion was that she should have paid a local to transport the medicine. They would have found a solution, and it's far easier when there is no *toubab* present.

"But I wanted to do everything correctly."

I don't consider myself particularly cynical, but I've now learned that it's often not possible to do things "correctly", and anyway, what is "correctly"? For me, getting the medicine to the hospitals is correct and there are times when it seems far better just to get the job done. Without giving those officials the chance to behave like madmen.

# DELTA DRIFT

*I've been stuck on an island for a couple of days now, spending much of my time lying on a threadbare plastic mat while I wait for a boat. These islands are mostly untouched paradises of white beach, forest and a smattering of villages that subsist by growing marijuana.*

*Bored, I stroll around the village, out into the mangroves and past a group of boys hacking up coconuts. They load me up with a few nuts, and I walk down to the river to break them open, drink the water and eat the fruit. When two dolphins glide gently past I decide that though I might be stuck, there are certainly worse places to get stuck in.*

*As I've seen throughout the islands, there are figures made from palm leaves and mounted on stakes, like scarecrows, placed all around the village. I later confirm with Khady that they are very powerful* gris-gris *called* jalang. *They protect the village – I'd often wondered why the authorities don't make problems, given the crop.*

*"They'd never dare. They'll die, and they know it," says Khady, referring to the powerful mystical beliefs to which almost everyone, police included, subscribes.*

The first time I trekked across the Casamance from the Gambian to Bissau borders was during the hot, humid beginning of the rainy season. Normally, in order to travel to Cap Skirring, the main resort on the coast to the south of the river Casamance and just north of the Guinea Bissau border, one must drive inland from Abéné to Ziguinchor, a journey of around 100 kilometres, then head west again, back to the coast.

The reason for not travelling directly down the coast lies in a massive delta system of islands, mangrove swamps and rivers, with precisely zero roads traversing it. There are several villages, mostly of the Karoninke tribe, a branch of the Diola who are Christians and animists.

The onset of Ramadan made it all the more tempting for me to get away from Abéné for a while. Although I'm impressed that virtually everyone unquestioningly abstains from even a sip of water throughout the entire day during the annual fasting month, I'm left feeling nauseous when I watch most people gorge on sugar and the equivalent of three meals in a couple of hours in the evening. Actually, it's a difficult time to travel, as everyone's on edge. Apparently, road accidents and fights increase dramatically – I can well believe it.

So I decided to hoof it across the delta with Fakeba, who'd never been to these islands before. We'd been working together for a couple of years by now, so this would be a great chance for him to understand a little more what I am doing, as well as an opportunity to get to know each other better.

We left in the early morning while it was still slightly cooler, although that didn't last long. Walking south along the beach to the next village we then headed inland past the charcoal makers and the cow herders, across dried-up rice paddies and on to the "port." In reality this was a shack in the middle of nowhere, near a dried-up, litter-strewn creek. An old toothless guy told us the boat to the island we were heading for left at 4pm, and it was by now about noon. So, we settled down on an uncomfortable log and swatted flies for four hours. Then we continued swatting flies for a further two hours, by which time the tide had risen and, along with a few other people who'd gradually gathered through the afternoon, we waded out to the boat.

After a lengthy boarding process, involving a very large trussed-up sow and then an unwilling, and if I may say, a highly inconsiderate cow that promptly jumped overboard, we were ready to go. I had been given the task of holding the rope to keep the cow under control, and I failed miserably.

We were only a few kilometres from a favourite swimming spot of mine, so I was slightly perturbed when, shortly after leaving, I spied a three-metre-long crocodile basking in the sun, mouth wide open to cool its brain.

This was the second time I'd taken this boat. On the first journey, the skipper had crashed into the mangroves, tipping several passengers into the water.

Which is precisely what happened again about two minutes after I'd had that recollection. Perhaps the skipper knows I'm an accidental African. The boat was having engine problems and it eventually cut out. The skipper lifted it out of the water and we drifted rather fast, straight into the mangrove roots, with no apparent effort to use the rudder. One passenger and a couple of bicycles went overboard.

Astonishingly, one of my friends who took the same trip shortly afterwards, also crashed in a similar way. Perhaps it's a daily occurrence?

There was a plus side. As we crashed, a troop of monkeys hooted and jumped from the very tree we'd hit, and I don't think we'd have noticed them had we just zipped past. I'm not sure the man overboard, who had by now been dragged back into the boat, was too interested in the monkeys, though.

We continued into larger channels and past pristine white beaches with little huts, arriving as the sun set at the island of Boune. I strolled through the sandy street greeting people. I could see Fakeba was impressed. Africans don't generally travel far outside their own sector, and if they do, they'll rely on help from trusted friends and family.

The first time I visited a remote village to the south of the Casamance, I arrived on foot after a 20-mile hike. I'd arranged to meet Khady there, and she was arriving from Ziguinchor, where she'd been staying with family. So, there I was, sweating, and drinking palm wine with a bunch of locals, when she arrived, chaperoned all the way to the meeting point by her bus driver, because, as she explained, she'd never been to this village before.

Perhaps it's wise for a young lady to employ a chaperone

in unfamiliar territories, but I have noticed the phenomenon also with able-bodied, strong, young guys, who become very timid when confronted with new geography and people. Maybe it's inevitable, given the low levels of literacy and near-universal incomprehension of maps. Whatever, Fakeba certainly looked impressed that "his *toubab*" was the one showing him around.

As Fakeba and I walked through the village, a girl handed us cashews, bats swooped overhead from a mango tree and boys played football in the sand. The owner of a small campsite there, Moise, remembered me from earlier visits. Small glasses of *cana*, the local rum, were poured, and we tucked into a large bowl of rice with oyster stew.

I also tried something I would never have thought of doing, a mixture of red wine and coke. It tasted like cough mixture, and although palatable, I'm not sure I'll go out of my way to retry it. Fakeba, a Muslim, didn't drink alcohol, but as travellers are exempt from fasting during Ramadan, he was taking water and small snacks during the day.

The Karoninke tribe are mostly Christian, having being converted by a Dutch missionary. They are related to the Diola but they have a different dialect. Beyond saying *kassumay* (hello, but here the response is *kassumay lama* versus Khady's *kassumay kep*), I don't follow this language.

In fact there are 11 dialects of Diola and some of them are about as different as Greek is to Chinese. For that reason, I've stopped focusing on Khady's dialect and am now trying to learn Wolof, which is how she communicates with other

Diola, and is viable across Senegal, The Gambia and even in parts of Mauritania and the Guineas.

Leaving Boune proved slightly problematic. There was a boat due to our next destination the following morning, but it was cancelled, so we spent the day exploring the village, checking out local *juju* fetishes – a collection of shells and bones strewn beneath a sacred tree where offerings such as palm wine are given to the spirits – and walked through a forest with a palm-wine tapper, who let me sample his wares.

"The boat will definitely leave at 10am tomorrow," said the boatman. Yeah. Of course.

We packed up and wandered down to the jetty, a little early, but I was happy to sit and watch village life.

Resigning myself to a long day, I strung up my travel hammock. I can never understand why people here don't make their surroundings a bit more comfortable. People spend vast amounts of time on very low wooden stools or plastic chairs when they could quite easily rig something up with some old rope and a bit of fabric.

But maybe I'm just a big soft *toubab* namby-pamby. There's no shortage of folk wanting to take my place in the hammock when I vacate it, mind you.

It was fun just lying back and watching village life go past, with a steady procession of people coming to shake my hand. I appreciate the politeness but continually having to explain my name and my surname and my father's name to people who clearly have no connection with any of us or any intention of retaining this information does become wearing.

Old men sat and stared at the water. Fishermen mended nets. Kids played in the sand. A few women flicked flies from the meagre goods for sale in what passed for a market. Chickens clucked and pigs rooted. By about 3pm, I'd had enough of village life.

I tried to get Fakeba to find out what exactly was going on, but ended up with weird explanations in his odd Gambian English.

"If I were to tell you the boat is going soon, is it that you would believe me?"

You get the picture.

So instead we sat and chatted about his early life in The Gambia. He surprised me when he explained that he'd been selected and sponsored as a child by a group of African Americans who had visited his village.

"It started really well and I had new shoes, American clothes, money for school books and food. But around me, people had nothing. You know, here there is too much jealousy. They hated me, and in the end I had to leave the village. That is why I never finished school."

It's just one example, but perhaps it would have been better to put the money into the school rather than singling out an individual, especially in a continent where individuality is not revered. I've worked in the charity sector in the UK, and followed the debate on whether one should give to an individual or to an organisation. I believe it should be the latter, although it's not so easy when confronted by real people with real problems.

The main thing to be aware of with any humanitarian endeavour – or in fact any endeavour – is that local problems can be unfathomably complicated, and what seem like simple solutions can on occasion lead to unintended consequences.

One guy I know here in Abéné receives around 100 euros every month from each of his several European girlfriends, all of whom are totally unaware of each other, while he sits back and no longer works at all. This could be an analogy for the aid model that creates a cycle of dependency.

Indeed, many Senegalese with whom I have discussed the subject believe that the aid culture keeps Africa in a childlike state, as opposed to giving its people a fair shot at sustainable development. Every household given just enough grain to keep them above the poverty line is a grain farmer who has just lost his clients. Suddenly, he's on the poverty line too, and the whole concept is self-defeating.

Despite the injection of many millions of dollars of aid money, it's a fact that more than a quarter of the countries in sub-Saharan Africa are poorer now than they were in 1960. Meanwhile, much of Asia, which received comparatively little aid, has lifted itself out of poverty through free markets.

Eventually the boat was ready. A group of young people was travelling to the village of Haere (pronounced "Hiya!") for a celebration. The people of Haere had come to Boune the year before, and I presumed it was some kind of matchmaking opportunity for these remote communities. I sat upon sacks of cashew nuts, barrels of palm oil and palm wine – Diola fuel. They also travelled with a full set of drums, which were set up in the back of the pirogue. As we set off, they started up, and played for the next hour or so, increasing the speed of the rhythm every time we sailed past any human habitation.

We left the main river, which was a kilometre or so in width, and turned down a small channel, at times so narrow that the mangrove trees formed a tunnel over its winding path. On the banks were piles of shucked oyster shells, sometimes 10 metres high.

We reached another river, the Kallisaye, and alighted on the opposite bank. The boat was continuing to Haere, our destination, but I wanted to walk as much as possible, even if Fakeba was finding it hard to understand the concept of walking for fun. As the boat pulled away, the drumming increased in ferocity and a woman started Diola dancing; a brave move in such a wobbly vessel.

There was a dilapidated set of fishing huts on a pure white beach. A bunch of filthy and toothless fishermen, already drunk on palm wine, were busy drying fish, and one of them, Jean, was walking to the next village, Bankesouk, so he accompanied us.

We walked across dried-up sand plains, then through shallow water, sometimes sinking into mud. One mangrove channel was thigh-deep. My mind wandered back to the crocodile, especially when something that sounded a little large for comfort swished through the water close by. After a pretty palm grove, we reached Bankesouk, an open, sandy village that somehow felt like the Wild West. Jean appeared to be in it for the long haul, so, after refilling my water bottle at the chief's house, we continued to Haere – a further hour or so through forest.

The first house of the settlement had a fetish covered in monkey bones, and a toothless, withered old woman crouched in the dirt beside it. I couldn't work out if she was mute, or just shocked to have a white devil show up on a Thursday afternoon. Just beyond were the youths from the boat, all banging away on their drums and looking surprised to see us.

We were led to the house of an elder, Dominique, the chief's brother. He sent out for two cartons of red wine, poured me a glass, and it seemed there was no question of where we'd stay. Good old *teranga*. They made up a room, showed us the shower, then poured more wine, this time mixed with Fanta. Fakeba seemed happy with straight Fanta. What more could we ask for? The answer, of course, was *bounok* – the Diola name for palm wine.

"Here's five litres, and have a bottle of *cana* (the local rum) too. How about a pig? What size would you like?"

I've eaten pork cooked in Michelin star restaurants, but this was the tastiest I've ever experienced, although perhaps the night sky, the *bounok* overdose and the fresh air also had something to do with it. While Muslim Fakeba had to make do with tinned beef, the rest of us ripped up hunks of meat with our fingers and dipped it into a mixture of French mustard, Maggi stock cubes and chilli.

By this point, 100 or more women had formed a circle and were clapping their bits of wood together manically while many people entered the circle, dimly lit by a fire, and danced the Diola flap, bent double at the waist, feet stamping up dust and arms flapping like lunatic birds. I reckon this is where Mick Jagger learned his moves.

It wasn't long before I was dragged into the circle, stamping up a storm, probably totally out of rhythm, but at least I tried. Each song sounded the same, but what a song.

One young woman sidled up to me, took my hand and attempted to drag me into the darkness. She was so stunningly pretty it was proving hard to resist. That is, until she smiled to reveal a mouthful of rotten stumps. I later crouched with other dancers for further rice and small, boiled river fish, drank some rather rank palm wine and then returned to Dominique's house and slept like a baby.

We were up with the roosters, and it's always a pleasure to watch the animals rooting around while the village kicks into action with the sunrise.

Dominique led us to a Belgian's house, quite literally in the middle of nowhere. A stunning little place. There were well-built mud-bricked buildings with thatched roofs, huge trees and a well-tended garden, all on the banks of a beautiful river, where a couple of sailing boats were moored off-shore. All of this was several kilometres from the nearest village, and the village at least 50 or 60 kilometres from the nearest place resembling a small town.

The Belgian, Yves, told us about his life there – a somewhat lonely life, unsurprisingly, and he wasn't sure how much longer he would stay. With almost no passing traffic, aside from me, he has little chance of customers, now that the French sailors and fishermen have stopped coming, due to the recession. Looking at the crocodile skins and other animal parts hanging on his wall, he sighed, and explained the environmental protection work with which he was involved.

"It's the local preacher. Every night he goes out in a canoe to shoot crocs. We're trying to stop him."

"Are there ever crocodile attacks?" I asked.

"I've only heard of one. A French guy, a crazy guy. He'd go out swimming alone around the mangroves at night. He came face to face with a big 'un, but he was lucky. It just took a chunk out of his bicep."

Like all proper mad-dog Englishmen travelling in the tropics, I dragged poor old Fakeba out shortly before noon, and we made our way onwards, walking through cute palm groves, across swamps, grassy plains and alongside rice paddies. By now, the villagers were Diola-Cassa, speaking yet another dialect (this time they greeted us with *kassumay ballet*), although I was still able to impress and raise laughs with Khady's Diola-Bouluf dialect.

Hitou was a small village on the edge of mangrove and impossible to leave except by boat or via the route we'd marched in by. In Haere, everyone had assured us that getting a boat would be easy. Approaching Hitou, folk started to look concerned, saying there's actually only one boat, and that it had left that morning to Ziguinchor. I asked at the house of the boatman and he confirmed the story before pulling up a chair, asking whether we wanted lunch and then providing mangos, boiled eggs, rice and fish. *Teranga* forever!

A familiar story: the boat would arrive at 2pm, then we could go. Four pm arrived, then 5, then 6. I was a little frustrated. Every time we'd got on a roll with walking, we were then halted for hours, or even days, on end.

Palm wine was served in the evening and I sat chatting to a lad who'd been schooled in The Gambia.

"I want to be a father." I was confused at first, as he was only 12 or 13 years old. Then he continued, and I realised he meant a preacher man, not a dad.

As per normal, there was no question that we wouldn't stay with this family. Can you imagine turning up at a village in Europe and being invited in, as a complete stranger, for multiple meals and to sleep overnight? I always pay something, but nothing was demanded and it's just normal African hospitality. *Teranga* rules.

I sat greeting people while eating grapefruits picked straight from the tree under a full moon in the African sky. There was no light pollution, no noise pollution, and in fact, given the lack of shops, no pollution whatsoever. Everyone seemed well-fed and happy, friendly without being overly curious; the perfect combination.

But it was a weird night. I awoke in the early hours with someone sitting on the window-sill shining a light around. He quickly ran, then the pigs started fighting, as odd bubble-like lights floated around the room. Perhaps there was something in that *bounok*? Rats and bats scurried across the corrugated zinc roof, keeping me awake until dawn, at which point chickens appeared in the room. Then the place came alive with the sound of animals, cock-a-doodle-dooing, sweeping and the chatter of children. Africa's wake up call.

I went and sat out with Grandpa, who was tucking into a filthy bucket of *bounok*, and I've long maintained that you can't beat a *bounok* breakfast. We were then presented with a platter of very greasy and sinewy chicken in onion sauce before a long wait for the boatman, who'd returned late the previous evening. Kids played with bows and arrows as I sat sweating. It was 8am and touching 40° Celsius.

The boatman finally turned up, and we waded out through a mangrove channel to his boat, then gently puttered out to the main river Casamance, which is several kilometres wide at this point, like an inland sea. Although a strong swimmer, I sometimes feel slightly vulnerable in such a small craft on such a large body of water.

I couldn't help but imagine being one of maybe a hundred or more souls crammed onto what is essentially a large canoe, bouncing up and down in the Atlantic waves bound for Europe, all of the hopes and all the savings of the village invested in the ride, but unable to swim should tragedy strike, as it inevitably does.

I mentioned my thoughts to Fakeba. "Why are young Senegalese and Gambians so desperate to get away? It's beautiful here, you're not hungry, you don't have to work so hard, you have plenty of time with your family and friends, and I can see how proud you are of your culture."

"Yes, but here's paradise for the white man, but for the black man, all is struggle."

He was repeating a line I'd heard many times. Most people in the world are aspiring for a better life, greater work opportunities and a more affluent lifestyle. Pretty much everybody I spoke to, including Fakeba, knew a few lads who were trying their luck, and I'd no doubt he'd go as well, were he not working for us.

Life for the typical young person may not be easy and there aren't so many jobs, but it's not impossible to have a decent standard of living and gain a trade. I personally think I can have a better quality of life here with £2 per day than I could in England, but of course, I'm easily pleased, and happy to be largely rid of the materialistic system I've seen in the West. I have experienced and then rejected this, however. It's easy for me to make an informed choice and, well, let's face it, keep the good bits.

Khady's opinion is that many people are lazy and want an easy life, for example to marry a white or to go to Europe, where they believe everybody is rich and life is easy.

"They need to change their attitude," she says. "They're

lazy, they're selfish and they'll always be poor. You're lucky; you were born in the *toubab* lands. You have a head start, but I see how hard you *toubabs* work. We need to take some responsibility, not keep blaming others for our problems, not sit around waiting for the *toubab* to give us money. That is, unless we want to always be poor."

"How much can you earn in a day in England?" asks Fakeba.

I guessed that an unskilled labourer may earn £50.

"See! A labourer here often won't get that in a month."

I tried to explain that there's tax, national insurance, transport, the cost of meals, rent, council tax, warm clothes and so on. Fakeba made the right noises, but his eyes were glazed. He'd only heard £50, and he probably thought the rest would be negotiable, as it is here in Africa, and  was forgetting he would be unlikely to have his Gambian-style family support systems.

It's also the case that local Africans who have been in Europe do not always speak honestly about the problems they – and we – have there. There's huge family pressure to return to Africa laden with expensive Western gifts and giving the impression that the streets are paved with gold. As with the rest of the world, there's a perception that materialism, consumption and having the latest i-whatever will bring happiness.

So, when a friend returned from Europe with several secondhand mobile phones for his Senegalese wife's children, they were happy. Until the following week, when her sister arrived from Paris loaded with original brand-new smart phones, tablets and more, at which point the secondhand ones were discarded. This sister works as a janitor and must have crippled herself to come back appearing rich and perpetuating the myth that everyone is rich and life is easy in Europe.

Our thoughts and conversation were interrupted when I glanced up to see a school of leaping dolphins. Before long we were coming ashore on the island of Karabane, a popular tourist place and an old French colonial trading station.

On arrival, we briefly strolled through the village, past a big, old French church that looked semi-ruined and mouldy in the tropical humidity. There was a military checkpoint next to it and a soldier sat with a machine gun – an image that at a glance reminded me of a scene from a Vietnam war movie.

The rains were coming, I felt hot, I was tired and really hungry after several days of very basic rice and fish. We went to a nice-looking hotel and I ordered first a coffee followed by an exceedingly cold beer – my first in a week or so. It hit the spot. It was the first sign of modernity and tourism since leaving Kafountine, and I sat feeling decidedly shabby in my dirty hiking gear.

The waiter proudly handed us the menu and I salivated over the myriad choices. I made a request, but it was not available. Neither was my second choice. Nor the third. After running through the entire menu, it turned out that only two items were actually on offer, although the waiter hadn't thought to tell me that beforehand.

On we went, continuing across further mangroves to the western edge of the island, with the intention of hiring a fisherman to take us back to the mainland. Instead, I got us lost. I'd taken this route before, but a newly built house confused me, I took the wrong path, and before long was wading up to my chest in swamp water while thinking of crocodiles. My brain's good like that.

When I felt my feet sinking into mud, fearing for the safety of my camera, currently in a bag on my head, I turned back, only to see Fakeba had followed me. I was touched to see that he was reaching out to me with one hand while holding his machete for the snakes and crocodiles in the other.

Back at the new house, I asked some girls who were shucking oysters the way. They led us across their garden to a communal boat on a rope-pulley system, upon which we pulled ourselves across a creek.

The beaches on the western edge were wide and wild, with cows, pigs, red flowers and plenty of palm trees. We walked to some fishing shacks and negotiated a ride across the one-kilometre-wide channel back to the mainland and the village of Nikine.

As we approached the shore the boatman stuck his hand in the water and fished out a reasonably large fish. Just like that. The Casamance is the land of plenty; it really is. On we went on our longest day of walking.

We finally reached the Atlantic shore and started down

the beach past picturesque washed-up trees and herds of cows. The Ziguinchor to Dakar ship sailed out of the mouth of the Casamance river and headed out to sea beneath a huge black storm.

The storm hit shore but on we marched, our eyes barely open against the pounding rain and wild wind. I raised my head and howled to the heavens, drenched to the skin. That was perhaps the most joyful moment of the whole trip.

The final few kilometres were tiring but exhilarating. The sky lit up every shade of orange, red and purple, while lightning flashed in distant storm clouds. I aimed for my friend Eddie's shack in the mystical Diola village of Djembering, and we arrived just after dark, the sky still flashing with lightning.

There are a few Europeans with colourful characters living around the Casamance, and my friend Eddie, who lives on the beach, is no exception. I found him celebrating with the village elders, as he'd just been made an honorary chief of the village. Over glasses of *bounok*, Eddie explained exactly why he prefers Senegal to Dublin.

"Everything's better here. Last night I chased cows. Something bit me in the night. Maybe a scorpion or snake; I'm not sure. But, I was still alive this morning, so who cares? I'm a fighter."

I'd timed our arrival in Djembering very well. The next day, Eddie had arranged for 150 men to prepare his land in the traditional manner, and to sow rice. He'd arranged a pig, a goat and 400 litres of cashew nut liqueur for the occasion.

We were now on the fourth and final type of Diola dialect of the trip (*kassumay jang*). Everyone wanted their photo taken and men started racing each other, forming small groups, chanting and acting out small plays, brandishing knives, as they worked with their traditional Diola spades. I ate hunks of delicious tender and 100% free-range pork with my hands, and drank *cadeau* from the bucket as it was passed around the circle.

I returned to Eddie's, and as I entered his shack, a topless Ukrainian woman handed me a cold beer and platter with crabs and huge prawns the size of my hand. As I looked out to the endless stretch of empty golden sands and blue waters, I decided life probably couldn't get much better than this.

"It's good now, but we've had problems. There was a thief, a local crazy, and for months no one could stop him; he'd just disappear into the forest. In the end the police came with guns. They shot at him but just blew his jaw off. That didn't stop him and he kept on stealing."

I had visions of this unstoppable "Terminator"-like character, missing his lower jaw, tongue flapping down onto his neck like a creature from a horror movie.

"Finally the army caught him, and he's in prison now. We can sleep again."

Later on were *lutte* matches, the traditional Senegalese wrestling. It's more than just wrestling, also providing a matchmaking opportunity: the young local men, fit and strong after working in the rice fields, show off their strength and prowess to the ladies.

I've seen plenty of *lutte* before, and it's always fun, but I was unprepared for this. As I crossed the brow of a hill, the only one in the region, I was greeted by the sight of a couple of thousand people spread down the slope around a central clearing surrounded by giant *fromager* trees, like a scene from the movie *Avatar*. The warriors, wearing loincloths and wrapped with *gris-gris*, chanted, stomped, whistled and marched in formation, surrounded by women liberally sprinkling talcum powder over them. One district of Djembering was fighting the nearby village of Kabrousse, and the two teams took their places on either side of the arena, along with their cheerleaders, who brandished large palm fronds.

Before the fighting started, warriors danced into the arena, flexed their pecs, growled at the opponents and forcefully hurled daggers into the ground. A display of aggression aimed to intimidate.

The *lutte* itself didn't take too long. Small boys fought, then teenagers, then the young men. The entire forest seemed to erupt every time there was a winner, and ladies ran into the arena, thwacking their palm fronds against the ground and spaying their men with talc. Occasionally a match would be deemed too violent and stopped. Other times you could almost feel the thud as bodies hit the ground.

Then, as quickly as it had begun, one of the village chiefs

ran into the middle, made a speech and everyone made to leave.

I walked back through the village, where the warriors gathered around large drums, and then the stomping and chanting resumed, to a primal beat. As darkness fell, Eddie and I retired to a nearby house where cauldrons bubbled over fires. Large enamel bowls were distributed and we scooped grubby handfuls of rice and pork that fell apart and dripped grease down our arms.

Eddie is a fighter and sat up drinking more *bounok*. I'm not, and as the celebrations continued I returned to his shack in the dark, stripped off and jumped in the sea. As I splashed in the surf, the water glowed with phosphorescence, created by a kind of plankton that lights up when agitated. It's magical, like being surrounded by fairy lights. What was more, the sky was lit up by regular flashes of lightning. I was truly in wonderland.

Khady was missing me and it was time to head home. We took breakfast, and as I watched Fakeba stir his customary five spoons of sugar into his weak coffee, he thanked me.

"I can't believe you're showing me these places. They're the lands of my ancestors and I'm the tourist here."

I certainly felt we'd bonded and looked forward to many more years of working together.

"But one thing before we go."

"What's that?"

"*Lutte!*"

Oh crap. I used to go to judo classes as a kid and more recently practised karate, but I wasn't sure I was ready for such a humiliation with a Diola. Most young guys here don't have an ounce of fat, and are pure muscle with rippling six-packs born of hard labour morning till night since childhood.

"Okay, you're on…"

We went down onto the beach, both wearing just our shorts, and squared up. Me, the awkward and out-of-condition, pasty white *toubab* and him, a lean, mean Diola fighting machine.

For a few seconds we lunged at each other, then he came at me charging. I sidestepped, twisted my body and gripped his arm, feeling solid knot-like muscle slamming into me. I'd been playing, but now I was in the moment, I was back at school fighting the bully, in the judo tournament beating my brother…I pulled him down, somehow got him in a headlock and held on as tight as I could.

"You win, you win! It's okay, we are brothers now; black and white, we are all one."

I'm sure he'd let me win.

I had one more quest on the way back to Abéné. In the town of Ossoueye, heart of the south Casamance Diola lands, there is a king, and if you proffer a little *bounok*, you can rock up and meet him.

How exactly do you secure an audience with a king?

Simple: you ask the guy tending the petrol pump next to the town garage. I did so, and a little later Monsieur Pompidou led us across the road to a huge baobab tree.

"This tree is just 20 years old," he said. "The ground is very fertile." Yikes, my Little Baobab tree is starting to turn into The Medium-Sized Baobab, and if it grows like this one, it'll soon be huge. Beside the tree is a black hole leading into forest, through which we passed.

It felt like a suitable entrance to an animist king's palace. We walked through the neatly swept dark passage and were told to sit on a log next to an old lady, waiting patiently with her offering of a 20-litre plastic barrel of *bounok*.

After a few minutes we were beckoned into the royal court, a lovely, neatly swept space under a large tree and surrounded by a fence of palm leaves. The king, known locally as Mam Sibiloambaye, was waiting. He shook hands, then sat on his low wooden stool, while brandishing what looked like a wand made of twigs. I sat opposite him on a plastic chair.

Monsieur Pompidou explained a little about the animist beliefs and the king's role, which is to mediate local issues and act as a peacemaker. Indeed he'd instigated the annual *lutte* festival to bring all local villages together as part of the Casamance peace process.

All the while, the King sat slumped, looking frankly a little less regal than I'd have hoped. It was only towards the end, when I mentioned Khady and my life in the Casamance, that he perked up, smiled and warmly took my hand, wishing me very good luck for the future.

Later we raced mile after mile in the bush taxi over potholed roads and corrugated red mud tracks.

Inside: hot diesel fumes circulating the cabin, dust coating everything, neighbours' elbows digging in, sweat dripping. Outside: bleached-out landscapes, burned scrub, magnificent trees, donkeys, carts, lethargic women swatting flies from fish stalls and lonely villages of small thatched roundhouses. Perfect. While not averse to luxury travel, there's a part of me that's never happier than when I'm experiencing massive discomfort in down-at-heel surroundings. It feels like the real Africa.

# ISLANDS ON THE EDGE

*"Come with me; there is a bar. With alcohol, with girls and skirts." That's the kind of invitation I can't refuse, so off we go.*

*The bar is in a shipping container in the port of Bissau. In fact, there are shipping containers converted into shops, restaurants and bars, across the nation of Guinea Bissau. This one is full of fishermen, many from Sierra Leone and Liberia, so I can chat in English and drink cana, a local rocket fuel produced from sugar cane.*

*There are indeed a couple of girls, both wearing tree-bark skirts. They are from the Bijagos islands. For years, I've heard snippets about the remote and mysterious tribes living on these islands. The few travellers I meet who have been there, speak of them in hushed tones.*

*One girl starts dancing, swaying sensually and rubbing her naked breasts against me as she holds out half a coconut shell that hangs round her neck. With trembling hands, I pour in a little cana, which she drinks before holding her head back, closing her eyes and softly wailing. Either this is a very unusual tribe, or she is mentally unstable.*

As with much of the continent, countries in West Africa were formed where colonials drew lines on the map. They rarely corresponded with ethnic, linguistic, cultural or historical boundaries. The Diola are centred in the Casamance, but are widespread throughout The Gambia and Guinea Bissau as well, and I often feel their culture is closer to that of Bissau than to that of Dakar.

Guinea Bissau has one of the world's lowest GDPs and ranks low on the human development index. The president was assassinated in 2009, in one of the few recent cases of a governing head of state being hacked to pieces. His palace in the centre of the city still had a bombed-out roof the first time I visited the place.

Its general lawlessness, its location and the treacherous nature of its archipelago island coastline have made Guinea one of the major trafficking points for drugs from South America into Europe. According to the British foreign office, "not many Brits go to Guinea Bissau". There may be good reasons for that.

The countryside is beautifully green and tropical and the people friendly, but the official insanity is something else again. My driving licence problems on the Guinea/Senegal frontier were the culmination of a trip filled with crazy official interventions that very nearly stopped me from ever going back to Guinea.

Actually, I should have taken the border crossing on our way into the country as a warning of things to come. I was stung for three times the normal fee for crossing a border in a private vehicle. It wasn't long before we reached another checkpoint that demanded our papers and a fee for stamping them. And on it went, every few kilometres a new checkpoint, a new stamp and another fee, usually extracted after I'd been dragged into some dingy room with peeling paint and an ancient fan stirring the soup. The critical thing is to remain very calm and positive when dealing with petty officials, because they are apparently *immensely* important, and irritatingly powerful.

When we crossed paths with a convoy of Spanish rally cars coming from the other direction, the drivers looked thoroughly miserable – another sign perhaps that this would not be an easy trip. About halfway to Bissau city, we were stopped by a couple of 'policeboys'. The first thing they asked me was to test the bulb illuminating the rear licence plate. I hadn't even realised there was such a light, but thankfully it worked. Then they asked for the fire extinguisher. I had one, as I've been stung for that before. They examined it and pointed to the expiry date – the end of the previous month a couple of days earlier. No matter how well prepared you may think you are, Africa's gonna get you.

"Twenty three thousand cfa," which is about £30. After a lengthy discussion during which the boy stared away from me impassively, fluttering his hand as if drying nail polish, he accepted 5,000 cfa.

There were police, military and customs checkpoints at every mediocre-sized settlement along the route, which meant every 10 kilometres or so, and they all asked me for the same amount: "douze mille". In French, this means 12,000 cfa. At every one I spent an average of 30 minutes arguing and fighting, driving myself crazy and eventually settling for 2,000 cfa. I'd hand it over with a weary sigh to their complete and utter confusion...because "douze mille" in the local creole language means 2,000 cfa. What a pillock I am.

Later, a friendly official explained that the police hadn't been paid for four months, which helped us to understand, but a smile and some banter while ripping us off would have sweetened the experience somewhat.

Just outside Bissau city, there was a big barrier across the road, with plenty of police and military officers standing around looking very excited to see a car full of tourists arrive.

A large, gappy-toothed policeman in wraparounds, clearly hungry for his slice of *toubab* pie, demanded my licence and insurance, and then took a look for several minutes, holding them upside down. Literacy rates in the region are low, even among professionals; they generally hover around 50%.

"These are not the correct papers. You will come with me and you will pay more money," he said.

"Okay," I replied, trying to remember my own advice and remain calm.

It transpired there was nothing at all wrong with the papers but he kept searching for an excuse to extort something from me, thankfully not noticing the expired fire extinguisher. Thank goodness the checkpoints are disorganised and probably don't have the phone credit to call ahead. In the end, he demanded the chassis number, so I told him to look for it, and after about 20 minutes of searching in vain he finally gave up, rudely telling me to be on my way.

Before I had left Abéné, Khady had presented me with two new black *gris-gris*, to be worn one around each upper arm as protection against police checkpoints.

"Under no circumstances let the police see them," Fakeba had warned me.

"What if they try to cause me a problem?"

"But they won't," he replied, perplexed how I could think such thoughts with the powerful *ju-ju* in hand.

How much worse could it have been had I not worn them? I reckon I'd have been better off chasing hornbills, though.

Sometimes I'm tempted just to drive through these roadblocks. After all, what could they do? Then, reading a Gambian newspaper, I found out. A taxi without the correct paperwork had accelerated through a military roadblock, so they opened fire, killing the passenger, a teenage charity worker.

After about four hours, and with a much lighter wallet, we reached Bissau. I negotiated the heavy traffic and managed to find my way to the old town near the port, where we found a room in a crumbling building and drank some Portuguese beers. It's an atmospheric city, population just 400,000, with crumbling colonial architecture and a similar feel to Goa, or Maputo in Mozambique – other old Portuguese colonies I've visited.

As I took a picture of the Grand Hotel, a man whispered

"be careful" in Portuguese. Groups of men sat around ghetto blasters listening to Guinean pop. It was highly rhythmic and I couldn't help slowing my walk, relaxing my shoulders and bobbing my head a little. This caused huge cheers and high fives. Had the street not been so potholed, I might have turned round and moonwalked.

As we were driving in downtown Bissau, one of my guests, Ian, took some pictures of the crowded streets. A policeman spotted him and hauled us over. Relieving me of my car papers, he and a colleague walked off and stood glowering at the traffic madness. Showing them we had deleted the pictures made no difference.

"Twenty thousand cfa".

I pleaded, but they just scowled at me. I made a potentially very dangerous mistake when, patience withering, I snapped, and made a grab for the papers. Quick as a flash the *gendarme* grabbed me, twisted my arm painfully up behind my back and marched me back to the car, reaching in and taking the keys.

I panicked, imagining myself being thrown into a dingy Guinean cell. I kept apologising, but my captor, who must have been 15 or 20 years younger than I, held me tight, while staring away expressionlessly. After a few minutes that felt like a few hours, he snatched the 5,000 cfa I proffered and pushed me away as if I were an annoying dog. I was free, for now. Thankfully, my guests, Ian and Alan, were perfect travel companions, and took it all on board as part of the African travel experience.

The three of us had also attempted to visit the Bijagos islands, an archipelago located a few hours offshore from Bissau city, but the ferry wasn't running, and even hardcore West Africa travel nuts had warned me against taking the local canoes for the six-hour trip across open ocean, so we had to abandon the idea.

But I had often thought back to the girl in the grass skirt from these islands, and from all that I'd heard, they seemed otherworldly, so when Khady decided to go to Dakar for the funeral of her father's second wife (this was the co-wife, not Khady's mother), it seemed a perfect opportunity for me to make the trip.

The journey began and ended with dolphins, and that's the way I like it. As I rolled into Ziguinchor from Abéné in the early morning, they were leaping from the river under the bridge.

I went straight to the Bissau embassy, where a man sat typing on an antiquated typewriter, with a packet of 100-hour Viagra coffee next to him. I must say, he did look suitably knackered. Five minutes later, brandishing a shiny new visa, I went back to the *gare routière* and jumped into a *sept places*, which, as soon as the driver had tied the exhaust back on, departed.

My Portuguese friend Miguel had told me that, following elections in early 2014, things were picking up in Guinea Bissau. Business regulations had been relaxed (it used to take

12 months to register a new business) and entrepreneurship was flourishing. Apparently, the roadblocks and corruption I'd experienced there before were now a thing of the past, and there was a new optimism.

At the border, I noticed a picture of the new president framed above the counter, although, every time I've crossed, it's been a different person up there, staring stiffly at the camera. We crossed fairly casually, then about 100 metres in, there was a roadblock. It didn't affect us passengers but the driver looked flustered, reached for his papers and a wad of cash and disappeared for ten minutes. And thus it continued all the way to the city. So much for the reforms.

Two or three hours later, we were approaching Bissau, a city that, despite its problems, always gives off good vibes, with its orange terracotta-tiled roofs, green rolling hills, bush in the middle of the city, appalling roads, *zouk* rhythms and people ready to party at the drop of a hat. Within about two hours, I'd been offered prawns, ice-cold beers and a couple of other things that could have made for a great time.

Later I went to a roadside bar and ordered a draft beer, which tasted like Vietnam's *bia hoi* (very fresh local beer) as the sun set and the mosquitos whined. I noticed a guy I recognised at the next table, Miguel's friend Andy, a German rasta I'd met a few months previously in Kafountine. I went over and he invited me to join his group. We were soon joined by eight or nine other Germans, some doing business and some missionaries, who all very politely switched to English, despite it being their German expat night.

"We have many immigrants coming to Germany right now, so no problem. We welcome you."

We had a great time drinking *caiprihinas* made with the local *cana*, which nearly knocked me out. Andy, who lives here, and makes his living with a *toca-toca* (g*eli-geli*, or in English, a minibus used for local transport) told me more about the current set-up.

"Yes, everything was going well, but the president had disagreements with the prime minister and fired him in August. There was a coup d'état in September. We are now having the third prime minister in one month and everything's turned to shit."

So, business as usual for Guinea Bissau.

I hit a nightclub later, and as the ubiquitous Nigerian and Congolese pop blared, I was approached by more hotties. Am I just phenomenally attractive to beautiful women or were they desperate? I suspect the answer is not the one I'd prefer.

"Hey, *branco* (Portuguese for white)…you have wife in Bissau? No? You want one?"

Even persistent rejection met with a spirited response.

"Ah, you have a Diola wife. Let me talk to her, I'm a Diola. I can explain everything and she'll want me as your second wife, for sure."

After a night in a small pension, not fancying the ubiquitous sweet pastries and not having eaten the previous evening,

I ate chicken and chips at a Lebanese place called Ali-Baba's. I'm pretty confident that every West African city has a Lebanese chop shop called Ali-Baba.

Around lunchtime I headed down to the docks to catch the ferry to the islands, which, after a couple of years of maintenance, was finally running again. I clambered over ropes and luggage to board the rusting ship, met a couple of other travellers and proceeded to drink a few small super-bock beers, eat a *bifana* sandwich and chat.

Aside from the moment one of the staff turned on the music – ear-splitting electronic noise so diabolical that everyone cheered, including the locals, when the Swedish girl I'd been chatting with ripped the wires from the speaker – it was lovely.

It was five hours across the ocean, sailing past several islands and sandbanks backdropped by an exquisite sunset. Lights appeared in the distance, and we gradually approached the island's capital, Bubaque. More a collection of ramshackle shacks than a capital, it felt like a pirate port to me.

Disembarking, I walked past the crowds (the boat arriving and leaving is an excuse for a party), past bars with cages across the windows and then up a deeply rutted mud track, where an eight-year-old boy called Wilson attached himself to me to guide the way through the pitch black.

I decided I was going to like this place.

The Bijagos are a collection of 88 islands set among 10,000 square kilometres of Atlantic ocean. Part of the archipelago is protected as a Unesco biosphere reserve. Several of the islands are home to the Bijagos people, one of the most isolated and secretive of all African tribes; some of whom have had only slight contact with the outside world. They have treacherous currents, tides and sandbanks, as well as the fact that villages tend to be set deep in the forests, to thank for this.

The Bijagos weren't considered pacified by the Portuguese until 1936, before which islanders made raids on ships along the African coast using their large canoes. I saw one such canoe with a platoon of bare-chested men rowing furiously, and even though I knew they were friendly these days, it felt intimidating. More recently, the region has been a major trafficking point for cocaine from South America, helped by the fact that it's pretty much the closest crossing point between the two continents.

The next day, I hired a bike and headed off to a supposedly idyllic beach on the other side of the island. Passing the faded grandeur of an old colonial Portuguese-style hotel that's rapidly crumbling into the jungle, I hit a "paved" road. To be honest, there were more potholes than paved bits, and a dirt track would have been smoother.

This ordeal lasted for 18 kilometres through jungle, small villages, rice fields, laughing children crying *"branco"* and a lake with a dead tree covered in the small nests and accompanying squawks of hundreds of bright-yellow weaver birds. No hornbills in sight. I'd been warned about the black mambas regularly found on the route, at times even jumping out of trees at people, but I was unlucky and didn't see any.

The road ended abruptly. One minute I was in the jungle, heartily singing "oh wimbo wey, oh wimbo wey," the next there was a crashing of waves and a steep drop down on to an empty beach.

It was almost idyllic... Palm trees: tick. The aforementioned white sand: tick. Warm blue sea: tick. No one else in sight: tick. Picturesque baobabs on the beach and photogenic dead fallen trees: tick. Sting rays: tick. Washed up medical waste: um...tick.

I counted seven needles and syringes as I walked along, slightly cautiously, wishing that I hadn't left my flip-flops back at the bike. I'd gone in for a swim, taking care to stamp the water ahead of me, as the region is notorious for the rays. Apparently, they hurt like hell and there was no medicine for the pain on Bubaque.

I found out that I could get a ride over to the nearest island, Rubane, which is visible from Bubaque, on the hotel staff speedboat that took workers from Bubaque every morning, returning after work. I arrived on the pristine beach, feeling weird turning up unannounced at a remote five-star resort.

It seems these islands attract two types of tourist: ragamuffins like me, who will happily rough it in a starless hovel and eat local food, and rich tourists, who are mostly here for game fishing and will happily pay 300 euro for a speedboat transfer to the mainland, and stay in five-star hotels. Some of them fly in from Senegal.

The hotel staff were lovely, especially when they realised I spoke a bit of Wolof. Very well-dressed French and Portuguese were heading from their rooms to fishing boats. Seeing as I was hitching free rides on the hotel's speedboat, I thought I'd better order something, so I organised some lunch, but first I wanted to visit the Bijagos villages in the forests behind.

I'd only walked about five minutes before meeting villagers who were stationed in their rice fields, scaring away the birds – even chasing hornbills, perhaps. They were astonished to see me and I soon realised that most *toubabs* didn't leave the confines of the hotel or game-fishing boats. Picturesque villages of straw and wattle were nestled among palms and rice fields. After passing through a dark tunnel of thick palm forest and mangrove swamps, I reached the first village. I entered via a gate with bunches of straw hanging from its top. I guessed – and later had confirmed – that these were protective talismans.

The first village appeared deserted, except for a mysterious agonising wail that was coming from one hut. I could hear other low murmurings, so I left them to it, continuing down a jungle track and crossing rivers of killer ants.

The next village was full of people who beckoned me over to sit on a pile of shucked oyster shells and chat, except that they barely spoke French, so I was a bit stuck. The poverty was striking, especially given that I had just left a five-star resort, but they seemed happy to see me.

I had a small wander in the rice fields and was questioned at every step. "What are you doing? Why are you here?" The people I met were genuinely curious, and happy to show me a little of their way of life, which appeared to consist mainly of scaring birds from the rice fields.

I felt bad going back for my luxury lunch, which was set out on a table on a wooden platform built out into the sea, and shaded by mangrove trees. I'd ordered just a main dish, not the three-course option, but they brought out a plate of miniature pizzas and slices of chorizo, saying it was a gift. I finished, and the pretty Côte d'Ivoirean waitress smiled and brought me a plate of Parma ham, salad and a glass of red wine that was perhaps half the bottle.

The inevitable question was soon asked: "Do you have a wife or girlfriend?"

"Yes, she's in Senegal."

"None here in Guinea? Now you have one!"

I started thinking that I may have been misunderstood, and they were bringing me the full multi-course meal, or perhaps this was part of the seduction, but I sure wasn't going to send it back. It had been a while since I'd had such foods. The main dish was a tower of tagliatelle with perfectly cooked lobster, tuna, crab, mussels and a creamy garlic sauce. They must have taken pity on me, as the bill was pennies.

Later, while whizzing back to Bubaque on the speedboat, wind in my hair, I felt full, but hungry for more knowledge about the mysterious Bijagos people. I knew that in order to learn more, I'd need to get to the islands without resorts.

Of the 88 Bijagos islands, only 23 are inhabited; the remainder are sacred and only specially initiated individuals may visit. If their secrets are revealed to those without the right to know, there may be serious repercussions both for those who reveal the secret as well as those who receive it. New secrets are given throughout a Bijagoan's life, until they reach the last beach, where a ship will take them to the other world, according to their beliefs. The secrets of the islands have led to the Bijagoans restricting access to them.

This has helped to preserve the land and its biodiversity, but is now becoming an issue, with the government giving contracts to foreign palm-oil producers and the encroachment of both industrial fishing and illegal Senegalese fishermen, who then cut the mangroves for smoking the fish.

I didn't want to upset traditions or trample around remote, untouched villages, so I arranged to take a public *pirogue* to Canhabaque, about an hour from Bubaque, inhabited and traditional, but visited by the occasional *branco*.

The trip started with a bad-feeling omen. As I boarded the boat, I sat on the edge, and the person behind me passed me a baby-sized package wrapped in cloth. As I took it, I realised it was in fact a baby. A dead baby. That explained the wailing and crying I'd heard for the previous 20 minutes as I was waiting for the boat. The mother took her seat, I handed back the baby feeling a little strange and disturbed, and then spent the next hour watching her constantly pulling back the cloth from its face so she could stroke and massage it and rub its eyes.

A little earlier I'd been sitting watching an angry dispute. A Bijagoan villager, probably in his mid-20s, was brandishing his carved wooden spear at others. His chest had a swirl of raised scars from his initiation ceremony, and on his head was a red hat like that of Noddy's pal, Big Ears. This slightly diminished his intimidating manner, it has to be said.

It was late in the afternoon as we crossed the sea towards Canhabaque. As we approached, I could see just a thin strip of pure white sand beneath a forest of palm trees. We approached an empty section of beach where people appeared, seemingly from nowhere, and some people got off to go to a village inland from there.

The sun was setting and the sky glowed first pink, then orange. The sea, a milky turquoise, seemed to glow slightly, and was as smooth as glass. The late afternoon sunlight burnished people's faces and behind me were among the most pristine white tropical beaches I've ever seen. If Bissau wasn't one of the least developed nations on earth, it would be thronged with sunbathers and five-star hotels.

I continued to the final stop, which involved travelling up a river through channels in the mangroves to a giant *fromager* tree, where the boat moored and dropped us all off. *Teranga* extends to Guinea Bissau and I'd already received several offers of a place to stay, but I ended up going with a Senegalese chap I'll call Moussa, as we were able to communicate in French.

If I was to draw an idyllic rural African scene, then this may well be it. The tree was a majestic giant, whose buttresses alone would dwarf a house. Monkeys chattered in the trees, swinging from vines, and scarified Bijago warriors carried their catches of fish from the water's edge and back to the village through dense forest.

Moussa led me through the forest to his house. We stopped at several of his friends' places along the way, each of whom offered us *bounok* and freshly roasted cashews, which drip from the trees in these forests.

As night fell, Moussa whistled, and there was a reply from the darkness. We came upon – and joined – a small group of men huddled around a fire deep in the jungle, all drinking ice-cold margaritas from salt-encrusted crystal glasses. Only kidding; it was *bounok* in cow dung-encrusted plastic mayonnaise pots. It's never tasted better.

Eventually we reached a small village of mud and thatched huts with no electricity – just the soft glow of candles. Mud houses with steeply thatched roofs blended into their surroundings with little distinction between earth and home. There was none of the usual corrugated roofing or plastic bags strewn on the ground.

"This isn't Europe," said Moussa, by way of an apology, leading me to a basic cement room with mattress and net that the village matriarch rented to me, but it was perfectly fine for this *branco*. I then sat fending off about 30 very excited kids and ate some bread with a couple of very large, fat cucumbers. Soft moonlight showed off the silhouettes of the palms all around me, and a Fula guy from Guinea, who ran the shop, pulled up a chair and a bottle of *sum-sum*. Although he'd spent time in The Gambia, neither he nor anyone else on the island spoke any English.

Sum-sum is a drink I've vowed never to touch. It's distilled cashew liqueur and, I discovered, absolutely foul. It's one of those drinks that makes people blind and often kills them, as I found out while Khady was pregnant with Alfie.

We'd been at the local hospital, getting a scan and being told she'd have twins. A friend of ours, Bienvenue, appeared and beckoned me over to a room. I entered, thinking he wanted a private conversation, and was shocked to be confronted with the dead body of a Frenchman, with whom I'd been on nodding terms in the village, laid out on a slab. It turned out he'd suffered liver failure following the consumption of *sum-sum*. So, on this occasion, I discreetly threw away the foul liquid from my glass when no one was looking.

Bellies full, we stretched out by the fire beneath the full moon, stars dripping down from the sky. The modern world felt a very very long way away, and there was even no sense of time. This could have been the 1800s, the 1700s or even the 1100s. As I lay there, thinking we'd landed in paradise, Moussa suggested that for under £500 he'd give me a piece of land with two houses and a wife. Under different circumstances I could have been seriously tempted.

The next day I awoke at dawn to the sound of cocks crowing and sweeping; the sound of probably every village on the continent. I chatted to Moussa, who got very excited when I told him about my guest house.

"You could build another one here," he declared.

"I'd love to, but one project is enough for me at the moment. Maybe one day." I couldn't blame him for trying, as it's probably not often he meets a *branco*, and those that come are often involved with humanitarian projects, or possibly drugs trafficking, in which case they'd have money.

I wasn't expecting much for breakfast, but I have to say it was a disappointment. Moussa brought out a covered bowl, whipped the lid off with a flourish to reveal...plain rice. Well, at least it was hot.

He told me a little about Bijagoan life. I enquired about the matriarchal system.

"Although the village chief is a man, women possess the power, manage the economy, social welfare and the law. They are respected as owners of the land and houses and they are responsible for constructing sacred buildings," he told me. I also gathered that descent is determined matrilineally, and often people don't know who their father is. Men are just turned to for hunting, farming and fishing.

The village was pretty. The women's traditional grass skirts and wooden bull masks hung from rafters. Very often in West Africa, I find the villages are pretty similar, and you wouldn't necessarily know it was Bijagoan from first impressions. Pigs, goats and chickens grubbed, kids followed me and ran scared when I chased them, women pounded grain with huge wooden pestles-and-mortars, adolescent boys and men sat around not doing much, with a bit of Afro pop tinnily playing from their phones (the village clinic had a small solar system where they charge phones). Apart from a minority of women who wore the grass skirts, most were wearing the typical wrap, t-shirt or vest and headscarf, while the males were dressed in ragged Oxfam clothes.

It's only at the ceremonies that the more traditional costumes come out. Moussa showed me to the church and the medical centre, where a pump donated by the Spanish had now broken down. Africa is full of broken-down donated Western technology, which has often been given without access to spare parts or the skills transfer necessary to continue maintenance.

After a brief dance and a merry sing-along with the ladies of the village, we set off for a longer stroll, Moussa striding ahead, rifle slung over his shoulder. I thought he might be planning on hunting, but when we met other villagers brandishing Kalashnikovs, I wasn't so sure.

I was geared up for a slog, but within 100 metres of leaving his house, we pulled into a neighbour's place, sat down and some *bounok* appeared. After a while, we walked on through the forest of huge trees and palms to three other similar villages.

We passed two forest clearings with bamboo goal posts set up. At the first, Moussa proudly told me this was known locally as Stanford Bridge. And the second was…wait for it, Wembley. There was no one there except a very old one-legged woman with a toothless grin and breath smelling of *cana* rum, who hugged me and seemed very excited that I was there.

Back in Moussa's village, we ate a traditional fish soup and then some rice with palm oil, while chatting about the possibility of my bringing tourists and using him as a guide. He explained that dances take place at numerous ceremonies associated with initiation, worship and the visits of important people. Various animal masks are made and violent dances performed, representing creatures such as bull, shark, hippo and swordfish.

He also said that if I bought 30 litres of cashew liqueur (fermented cashew apple juice, not *sum-sum*), the village would have a party in my honour.

"How much will that set me back?"

"3,000 cfa" – or about £3.50.

"Let's party!"

A fire was lit and the village drums were brought out. Some of them were placed with their skins in the flames, to tighten them. The women appeared in their grass skirts, half-naked and skin glistening where they'd rubbed in the deep orange palm oil. They began chanting, their shell-bound feet rattling the rhythm, and dancing in a circle around barrels containing the 30 litres of cashew liqueur.

The drumming seemed a little amateurish to begin with, but when they grabbed one of the fire-heated ones, it produced a thwack of twice the volume and the festivities intensified. The kids were wildly excited, and kept handing me what I thought was raw rice. When they weren't looking I threw it on the ground, but of course they saw everything and gave me more, indicating I should eat it. I'm still not sure exactly what it was. Some kind of roasted grain that sure wasn't great, but my handful was continually replenished.

Then the men, enormously muscular, dressed in sarongs and covered in leaves, commenced dancing. One guy who knew how to party, showed up wearing cow horns, a spiky puffer-fish helmet, whistles and bells, and all sorts of things hanging from his robes.

We danced away into the night and polished off the cashew liqueur, as well as a fair bit of wine. I splashed out and bought another 30 litres, and the entire village continued partying long after I'd gone to bed.

I returned from Eden to Bubaque, and told a bunch of guys I'd made friends with there about my great time with the hospitable Moussa. As I described the experience, their expressions changed. Wide-eyed with amazement, one of them whistled and mopped his brow.

"Wow, you're lucky; he's well known in these parts. Very well-known. A well-known killer."

I spent the rest of my days in the Bijagos resting, swimming on secluded beaches, visiting villages, thinking, writing and wandering around the bedraggled port area. I feel at home in slightly more down-at-heel surroundings, and relished just sitting with a coffee and watching the people going about their business. I slowly got to know the *sum-sum* drunks, the tattooed ladies and the eager Sierra Leonian, who I knew just wanted me to buy him beer.

Bubaque is a pirate town and the jetty is surrounded by rotting, caged drinking dens, (the best kind, surely?), huge jungle trees, into which locals have built businesses, kids shouting "*branco*" and a very large goose that padded about trying to peck at me. I heard people whispering "Americano" as I walked past, for some reason. I was staying up the hill, up a road that was more ravine than road.

Chez Raoul, my lodgings, had seen better days – faded Coca-Cola signs, peeling paint and an adjoining night club, but no power or generator. Raoul was an old chap with roots in Nigeria, Togo, Benin and Senegal. He told me he'd entrusted the place to a friend while making a trip, but when he returned, he had found it gutted, and he'd never quite had the means to re-establish himself.

Malaika the Nigerian was a former employee of the Senegal Experience, a UK travel company, a lovely guy who writes poetry in French in his spare time. He had a long tale of woe that led him penniless to the island, a prison from which he could not escape. As he led me to my room he issued me a warning: "This is not the Sheraton."

He was correct, but the mattress was firm, the toilet bearable and the sheets clean. That's enough for me.

In the evenings we'd sit outside under skies of a billion stars, with constant flashes of lightning, sipping *cana* rum and trading stories. Malaika had many theories, mostly gleaned from the works of Paulo Coelho.

"There's only one truth," said Raoul, a pastor as well as a hotelier.

"I believe there are many truths, but we all have our own reality," was Malaika's response.

"Perhaps there's one truth but we're all products of our own environment, our history, our culture, our communities.

187

We all just interpret it our own way," was my idea.

The local Bijagos people are nominally Christian, and Malaika confirmed my theory of African faith.

"You can Islamicise or Christianise an African but you can never take away the fact that he is an African. Everyone is still protecting themselves against witches and wizards, and they do exist. We Africans prevent our own development."

It was 2 November, Dide los Muertos or the festival of the dead, a Mexican tradition that's spread to other Latin American countries and presumably here via Brazil, which has a shared Portuguese history and affinity with Bissau.

Several groups of children were parading around the village; a boy at the front holding a candle while the rest banged bits of metal and chanted. They were begging for coins and I had none.

"It doesn't matter," said Raoul. "Give them a coin and they'll just spend it on sweets, then tell every other group that you gave. You'll be plagued all night."

When the third or fourth group made their demands, Raoul sent them packing. The Bijagos people do tend to look fierce, and I saw one teenager muttering, staring at me with hatred.

"They're insulting you," said Malaika.

"No, they're cursing you," said Raoul.

"I don't care, they're just kids."

"But you should. These islands are very dark; curses mean something."

Oops.

I went to bed and lay in the humid heat having crazy

dreams. At some point, I awoke. A clanking of metal and the banging of a drum, which sounded like a chain gang of crazy dwarves, was getting louder and louder. There was a frenzied chanting, right outside my thin corrugated metal door. Or was I dreaming?

Wiping the sweat from my eyes, I considered getting up. Perhaps I was missing a unique Bijagos cultural experience? Then something loud and metallic crashed into my door, I freaked and there I was, in my mid 40s, considering hiding under a blanket. But it was far too hot, so I just lay there, breathing shallowly, hoping I couldn't be heard, feeling very small, very alone and absolutely bloody petrified.

This is Africa. It is very dark here and there are many things I can never understand. But given that all I found outside my room the next morning were some small children's footprints in the dirt, I certainly can feel like a daft fool.

As I returned to the mainland on the ferry, we were followed by schools of dolphins. As I watched the sun sink into a sky awash with every shade of yellow, orange, pink and then purple, I vowed it wouldn't be long before I'd return to these magical islands. Even if that did mean getting terrorised by a bunch of kids.

# ONCE MORE INTO THE SWAMP...

*I am sitting on my verandah when the wind picks up. This is not a light breeze but a howl of spinning dust, of dried leaves and sand that blasts my face, while one of our 20-metre-high kapok trees is uprooted and crashes to earth, just missing the house. A huge boom of thunder makes me nearly jump out of my skin, and then it begins: the first rain. One second we are dry, the next it is as if someone standing above is throwing big buckets of water over us. Small plants are flattened; everyone runs around shrieking with fear or delight.*

*Except for where the electrician poked a wire through the roof, our straw roof is watertight. Where the unthinking workman made the hole, the bucket placed to collect the drip fills every two minutes.*

*Then Khady appears, a beautiful vision, eyes wide and grinning a euphoric smile as her soaking wet Union Jack t-shirt clings to her skin. Raising her arms to the sky, arching her back and head back, she drinks in the rain as the weeks of dust, rising heat and humidity, for a while at least, are washed away.*

*And once more, the swamp becomes a part of daily life...*

To love is to suffer, the things that bring the most pleasure in life can also bring the most pain, and for me, that sums up life in the rainy season. The heat and humidity build up to extraordinary levels. Roads wash away, houses collapse in the rain, crops are destroyed by waterlogging, and one day the village school roof blew off. Everyone in my family has minor but annoying bacterial infections and everything throughout the house is damp.

It is still my favourite time of year, though, which always astonishes those *toubabs* who escape to less torrid climes. Everywhere I go, I am offered the sweetest mangos I've ever tasted. I can just put some shampoo in my hair and run around outside for a warm but refreshing shower. I have a little respite from watering the garden, and everything glistens with startling clarity. There are 50 shades of green and I am still smiling, albeit through gritted teeth.

That said, there are still occasions when I am sorely tempted to leave, but of course I have a family, a business and responsibilities. I've made my bed and I'm lying in it – sweating, mostly.

Life during the monsoon certainly tends to be rougher even than at other times. The mud and the rains may seem to have played a disproportionate part in these pages because many of my hairiest adventures have been a result of monsoon conditions: the treachery of the swamp.

The Diola tribe is descended from the Feloops, which means the swamp people. They are referred to by Mungo Park as "a wild and unsociable race of people." Mungo travelled up the river Gambia searching for the source of the river Niger in 1795. Knowing how tough it is, even now in the age of motorised transport and when the locals can speak some English or French, I can only begin to imagine how it must have been 200 years ago. Mungo's journals are full of fantastic accounts of being robbed and left naked in the bush, of meeting kings with riches beyond those of Europe at the time, and encountering elephants, lions and other creatures that are now found here only in zoos.

I am reminded of the term "swamp people" when I recall one of the worst of all my monsoon misadventures...

Khady had gone to Dakar for a few days, partly to go to a good hospital to check out her ongoing health issues. This left me responsible for Gulliver, who was by now going to nursery school and due back home at midday. I knew that he'd be upset to find neither Khady nor myself at home, but I needed to pop up to The Gambia again to pick up some building materials. So I left early with Fitty Futta, intending to return in the early afternoon to be with Gully.

In retrospect that was a stupid plan. The first rule of planning in Africa is always to accept that the plan won't work.

But it started well, and we drove along the dusty red track past red colobus monkeys and a troop of around 30 baboons. We had to make purchases in Brikama and Jeswan, just to the north of Serrekunda, the main commercial city of The Gambia and just to the south of Banjul, the capital.

As usual, I sat around in wrecked old car and bus seats

with ripped upholstery (with high levels of apparent litter, it's easy to believe West Africa is an environmentalism dead zone, but actually very little is wasted), or on sacks of cement in oily and dusty corners of builders' merchants, while Fitty negotiated. Or I'd wait, sweating, hidden away in Kermit, as prices have a habit of miraculously increasing if there's a *toubab* in sight. Fitty can then take his cut unobserved, but it still works out cheaper for me, so I can accept that.

Shopping in Africa takes time. I sent Fitty off to buy me some phone credit. He returned, smiling.

"Did you get it?"

"Oui."

"Where is it?"

"All the shops had run out."

Oh dear, another African conversation.

Eventually, by about 1.30pm, everything was purchased and loaded, and it was time to head back. I should have been back with Gulliver by 3pm.

Then Fitty declared he had several other jobs. I didn't want to hang around, so we decided I'd leave and I gave him the fare to return by public transport.

"Don't go the way we came; the Senegalese military will make you fatigué. Go via Kabadio," he advised me.

"It's possible after the rains?"

"Yes. It's not rained for two weeks. You'll be fine," were his parting words. I would have plenty of time to ruminate on that particular nugget of wisdom...

I passed through Brikama with no problem and reached

the police checkpoint, where a policeman flagged me down, shouting "Simon!" It was Sherif, the policeman who'd fined me before for not wearing a seatbelt.

"But, you see Simon, now I am having a problem and I am needing you to help me."

It's tricky to refuse policemen and others in authority.

"I need a white lady, a boss lady, a *toubab* lady."

Promising to send one his way (message me through my website if you are interested) I continued to the border, crossing with no further problems. The chief of customs greeted me, uninterested in any of the goods in the back of the car (effectively, I'm a smuggler) but asking if I'd found anyone to help his school.

Last time I crossed here, I was taken into the back room of the immigration shack and sat down to be introduced to the chief. Scenarios like this are always a little bit worrying. Usually you're going to get shaken down and you have to weigh up how much time you have versus how much you want to give.

On this occasion, he gave me a very formal speech about a school in a nearby village, their lack of facilities and how they needed help from the West, in the form of money or books and other materials. I wasn't quite sure how to respond. I'm not against trying to help a school in need but there are plenty of scams here, and besides, it's not my country. Should I decide to get involved with a school, it'll probably be a Senegalese one.

I continued into the bush. No one gave me any indication

that the road wasn't passable, so I happily ploughed on like an imbecile. The first kilometre or so was fine and the sand had dried up. Then there was a slightly muddy patch, but it didn't look too bad. I pushed on a little way, then thought I'd better get out to check. I got down and decided that if I kept to one side then I would probably be okay.

While I was standing around making my assessment, the car sank. Oh, for God's sake, I thought. I'd been doing so well, and had spent the entire rainy season without getting towed out of a bog (unbelievable as that may seem, to judge from tales earlier in this book).

I put the car into four-wheel drive and tried inching back and forth, but I was well and truly stuck. I decided the easiest thing would be to walk back to the border post and try to round up some people and spades.

It was about 3pm, and I was about halfway back to the border post when I turned a corner on the muddy bush track and spotted a pair of Abyssinian ground hornbills pecking at the ground. There was a brief stand-off as we stared at each other, and then, before I could chase them, they turned and disappeared into the bush. I suddenly had a bad feeling...

I was dripping with sweat when I arrived back at the customs post, and pretty dirty from wading through the mud. I received some surprised looks from the border staff, but one chap, Morro, from the drug enforcement agency, issued some commands and a few minutes later we had four men, a rope and a jeep.

When we got back to Kermit, the driver simply huffed and

puffed, deciding it would be impossible to pull the Land Rover out. So, instead, we jacked it up, inserted logs and branches beneath the wheels and raised it to a point where we thought it should be possible to reverse out. No such luck. The wheels were stuck fast and I was going nowhere – equally fast.

There was nothing else they could do except suggest that I go to the nearby military camp, where there was a tractor. I was accompanied by Morro, who procured me an audience with the commander, a very friendly man who was happy to learn I was British.

"This is the difference between Anglophone and Francophone countries," he explained. "We will help you. On the Senegalese side they never will; they won't care. The British trained us to be friendly and care." Right, so if the Brits hadn't trained him to be friendly, he wouldn't be? was the question I didn't dare ask.

Darkness was falling and the soldiers wanted to say their prayers, which seemed to go on forever. Then they had to start the tractor, which needed to be jump-started. Ever tried jump-starting a tractor?

Finally, it was running and I sat on the back while someone looked for a torch, as the tractor lights didn't work. Then the commander returned, looking concerned.

"How far is the car?"

"Only 50 or 100 metres," said Morro. I knew full well it was more like a kilometre away, but I didn't want to give them a reason not to help, so I remained quiet.

"Is it on the Gambian or Senegalese side?"

"Definitely still in The Gambia," said Morro. This guy was fighting for me.

Apparently there were some border issues, relating to local marijuana plantations, and the Gambians were reluctant to get too close. I sat quietly, hoping I wasn't about to become responsible for an international incident.

They decided to send some soldiers with Morro and myself to check. If all was okay, they'd call the tractor.

So there I was, in the by now pitch-black African night, trudging through sand with a small platoon of heavily armed soldiers, worried out of my mind about Gulliver but completely helpless, as there was zero phone reception.

They didn't question the distance, but they did doubt the efficacy of the tractor. By now I had visions of leaving the vehicle there for weeks until the ground was sufficiently dry. Oh crikey.

My man Morro, drug enforcement agent extraordinaire, persuaded them to give it a shot. So, after an agonisingly long wait, they finally came, with just a crappy Chinese torch, supplemented by the light from my mobile phone. And after a little kerfuffle, they attached a rope and pulled Kermit out.

I was ecstatic. Now I could get home to my boy. I was pretty worried, and although I knew he'd be fine with Yama and the others, he would probably be crying and wondering where both his parents had disappeared to.

I offered some payment to the commander and Morro, which was refused. In the end they accepted a little something to buy *attaya* tea, but that was all. Morro gave me his phone number, told me we were now brothers and then directed me down a different track, which he assured me would be fine.

And it was – for a while. I hurtled along the sand tracks thinking of cool, cool water, a shower, Gulliver and a cheeky glass of red. I reached a fork, so I took the wider track, and continued for a kilometre or so until I found myself in a marsh. Hmmm, that wasn't good. It looked as if there was a track through palm trees to one side, which I nearly tried, but decided it was too narrow. If only I'd stopped, got out and investigated.

Instead, I reversed back the entire way to the fork, as there was no turning point. Then I continued along the narrower route, only to see another large puddle. I entered very slightly, thought better of it and got out to check, in exactly the same manner as the previous disappointment.

What a complete idiot. It was pretty huge with no sign of how deep it might be, so I climbed back in to reverse Kermit out, only to find I'd sunk again.

Had I not been dehydrated, I think tears would have flowed. As it was, water conservation physiology kicked in, and I just gulped like a gormless fish, contemplating a scary night in the jungle.

Unable to dig myself free, I decided to walk back to the last house and ask for a bed for the night and a bucket of water, both to drink and to wash off the slime. *Teranga* is strong. People usually have mosquito nets, and a night without one was not a pleasant thought. I had only 5% left on my phone battery when I set off from Kermit, and the torch drains it fast, but after walking for about ten minutes, barefoot in the sand, as my sandals were sodden with mud, I started to think that it was a lot further than I had thought, so made a snap decision to turn around and sleep in the car. It would be better security-wise and I could start again at first light.

By now, I was starting to think this was becoming a survival situation. I was gasping for water but figured I'd lick some dew from leaves. Unfortunately for me, they turned out to be bone dry.

I reached poor old bogged-down Kermit just as the phone battery conked out, but it wasn't as if I could have called, texted or Whatsapped someone for help. The modern digitally-connected world did not extend to where I was.

I jumped in, closing the door quickly to keep out the swarms of bugs, and cleared the back seat. I couldn't quite stretch out, but it wasn't too bad. No, I lie – it was rubbish.

My shirt was drenched in mud and sweat from where I'd mopped my brow, so I removed it to use as a soggy and ineffective pillow. It was still very hot and humid and I'd wound the windows up fully, as I could hear the clouds of mosquitos whining outside, and more than a few inside.

Incredibly, despite hearing that excruciating whine in my ears all night, I didn't get bitten. Perhaps the coat of mud protected me. I did have a very minor scratch on my arm, which the next day emitted an impressive quantity of pus, having been dunked several times in the primeval soup of the puddles in which I'd become trapped.

All lights off, I was all alone in the forest. I lay thinking about my predicament, sweat dripping all over my body, making rivers through the coating of mud.

A plan formed. I decided I'd try digging for one hour in the morning. If that didn't work, I'd walk to the next village, find a motorbike taxi to Abéné and then get Fitty "the route is fine" Futta and his friends to come, dig and return Kermit to me. Good plan.

By now, the jungle noises were almost deafening, and I watched the flickering of glow worms and fireflies. I had a bigger concern on my mind, though: bandits.

As I mentioned, these border areas are used as marijuana plantations and I'd heard talk of ex-rebels living in the forests. What would I do if I heard someone, or a car? Would I flag it down for help or hope they didn't notice me, which was hardly likely, given that I was blocking the path. I didn't have an answer, but felt nervous thinking about it.

Images from a horror film where kids get terrorised by a witch while lost in the woods flashed into my mind, as they always do when I'm alone in the wilderness. It's easy for the mind to play tricks when it's dark, and you are scared and alone in the jungle.

Years ago, I spent the night at the bottom of a gorge in Namibia, listening to what sounded like the ghosts of German soldiers encircling me all night long. The next morning, after I'd hiked 15 kilometres back to the nearest farmhouse, the German farmer's wife laughed and informed me that I'd met the resident aardvark, whose footsteps sound just like a man.

I've always maintained that if you think adventure is dangerous, you should try routine – it's lethal, but now I wasn't so sure. Not for the first time in Africa, I felt very small, very humble and very naive. I couldn't believe that here I was in November, when I could quite easily have been curled up under a nice thick duvet in bed in Brighton, having spent a lovely evening by my fire with a good bottle of red wine and a bowl of hearty and delicious stew. Perhaps I'd have watched a great film with friends and be looking forward to a relaxing weekend with walks on the Downs, darkness falling in the late afternoon as we retreat for a couple of pints of real ale in an old thatched cottage of a pub.

Instead, here I lay, alone in the darkness: damp, covered in mud, stinking and exhausted, with mosquitos whining, malaria imminent and bound to be robbed, or worse, by rebels. I listened to the jungle noises: the crack of branches, the croak of frogs, owls hooting, insects chirruping, splashing noises in the surrounding bogs. Could I hear voices? Was that the sound of footsteps? Dogs howled unceasingly in the distance, and I had the impression that something very bad was lurking in the forest.

Eventually I drifted off into a kind of mild drowse, and although I woke up every time I needed to turn – something it was impossible to do naturally on the cramped back seat – I must have had two or three hours' kip before the dull glow of dawn arrived.

I was somewhat alarmed to see footprints, significantly

larger than mine, right outside the car door, but there wasn't much I could do about that, as I had to get out of there before I died of thirst.

I jumped out, barefoot and bare-chested, and collected some branches. When the light was sufficient, I investigated and noticed that the differential was buried into the mud. The wheels were in two parallel trenches but hadn't yet sunk, as far as I could tell. There just wasn't enough clearance, so I was stuck. Okay, this looked promising.

I unloaded the 300 litres of oil containers that were weighing the car down considerably, jacked Kermit up, squirmed underneath and started digging the undercarriage free with a screwdriver, the only tool I was carrying. Here in Africa, I learn new lessons every day: carry a bloody spade.

I spent around an hour digging a trench with that damned screwdriver. When I dropped Kermy off the jack, everything looked to be free, so I prayed the wheels hadn't now sunk, and clambered back into my muddy torture chamber. As you know, I'm not superstitious, but I stroked my *gris-gris* and muttered a few words, went into four-wheel drive and stuck my foot down.

Joy. Kermit slithered back as easily as a knife through butter. Thank goodness for that. My mojo was back and my heart was racing with excitement and overjoyed with the thought of returning home to my boy.

I switched off the engine and then loaded the oil back into the boot, feeling proud for digging myself out of this mess. Usually car bog-downs take five or six people to dig, push and shove for many hours.

In I clambered, turned the key and...and nothing.

This couldn't be happening.

I tried again and the engine turned slightly, as if the battery was flat. There was a stillness in the air; I wasn't exactly swamped with people to push-start me, and I sat, my dry tongue starting to swell, tears unable to form, so instead I just gently mumbled.

I fell into a dazed, dehydrated slumber and started hallucinating. As I writhed and sweated, I had a nightmare vision of hundreds of huge, bloody red hornbills pecking at me, gnawing at me, in my ears, my eyes, my nostrils – every orifice going. They were cackling while I lay helpless, sprawled out in the jungle too exhausted to move or defend myself. Then there was nothing, as I drifted into oblivion.

Later, I heard a soft voice from afar.

"Kong kong," a local term used when entering a room or approaching someone you don't know.

I woke from my crazy dreams, lying in the mud beside Kermit, to find the distant voice was in fact right above me. I groggily looked up to see a filthy-looking local guy, pushing a bike with all the gear to collect *bounok*, leaning in and shaking my shoulder. Sadly for me, he was on his way to collect it and the containers were empty.

I'd earlier taken tentative sips from the dirty puddle but immediately vomited it up, and could now barely speak, but managed to give him some tatty African francs and the phone number for Fitty.

"Tell him I'm here, come quick," I whispered in rudimentary Diola, unsure whether the guy would bother.

A couple of hours later I heard the low rumble of a vehicle approaching through the bush. After an age, a motorbike rounded the corner, and I was astonished to see that the driver was Skippy, while Fitty was waving joyfully from the back, brandishing a bottle of water in one hand and some tools in the other. I nearly cried.

Gulliver screamed with joy as I arrived home. Apparently he'd cried till 3am asking for me. Yama couldn't believe I'd spent the night alone in the forest, for I'm a *toubab*. Surely it's not possible?

After drinking a bucket of water, I enjoyed a leisurely meal, drank several coffees and then took Gulliver to play on the beach for the rest of the day.

All was good until Khady called from Dakar.

"Simon, I'm fine but there's a problem."

There's always a problem. "Go on…"

"I was in the market. The thief, he take all my money. I have nothing. I can't feed Alfie, I can't come home."

She'd been pickpocketed and lost the 100,000 cfa (£130) that I'd given her for buying various things and sorting her passport.

How come it never rains?

# LOVING THE ALIEN

*We are watching the movie* Gravity *about a couple of astronauts fixing a satellite, who are involved in an accident and then struggle to get back to Earth. Khady and the others have no awareness whatsoever that man has ever been into space, landed on the moon and so on. I try to explain and they nod, um and ah, but clearly think I am making it all up.*

*Then we watch a fantasy sci-fi film,* Avatar. *I had thought it would be simple to understand and explain, as well as a fun film for Khady and the kids. Halfway through, Khady asks which country it is based in, so I tell her it is a fantasy film; it's all made up.*

*"Well, what's the point of watching it then?" she says, wandering off to do something more constructive.*

I never set out or expected to fall in love with a girl from an African village, with such wildly different background and values. In fact, I'd probably have laughed and thought it would never work, even though similar backgrounds, ideas and values had not actually proved much use in the long run for my previous relationships. Now, I'm at a different point of my life. A little older, a little wiser and a little more experienced. And things look a little different.

So, how do we manage to relate, and is it possible to make it work? I'm slightly wary of over-analysing, as I don't want to lay the magic bare, but needless to say, it's a different type of partnership to any I've previously had. Khady is my guide and my teacher in this strange world. We're never short of things to talk about or laugh at, but it's true that our conversations are very different from those I have with Europeans, and I maintain strong friendships with other *toubabs* to keep that type of conversation in my life, too.

Perhaps, to put it very simply, Europeans live by their heads, and Africans by their hearts. Khady doesn't seem to have the least little bit of curiosity about abstract things like ideas and distinctions. Maybe, by being with her, yet retaining my European friendships, I am getting the best of both worlds.

In earlier times in the West, marriage was a practical arrangement; there was no expectation that it should fulfil all one's dreams. These days, we demand everything from one partner: a lover, a best friend, a mother or father, a soulmate, and so on. Yet how can one person supply all those things? Most of the time they can't, of course, so we end up with a lot of unhappiness and unfulfilment, a nagging sense that there must be more to life, and high divorce rates.

My relationship with Khady is a far more practical arrangement, although it has the added charm that we do also love each other and have a lot of fun. But there is certainly also plenty of at times maddeningly different and difficult cultural crossfire to be accommodated.

Religion has always been perhaps the biggest elephant in the living room with Khady and myself. She's a Muslim and I'm typically British, in that I was raised nominally Church of England, but only ever attend church for the occasional wedding or funeral, and long ago lost my faith in organised religion.

I'm certainly not narrow-minded, and am always open to changing my beliefs if something occurs to prove them wrong. It's true that I've seen a lot of weird, inexplicable things here, but I still don't usually conclude that any mystical or magical event has occurred; simply that we don't have the means to explain it right now – much as a thousand years ago we had no idea the earth was round. In a couple of hundred years, many things we don't get now will probably be understood by the knowledge of the time. Giving a mystical explanation seems to me to be an admission that you haven't a clue.

But I recognise I'm speaking as a Westerner, with a totally different way of thinking, including a freedom to choose what I believe. Africans are, almost without exception, very strong believers, and to reject their faith would lead to ostracism by family and society. So, given that family support is crucial to survival in a region of such high poverty, why would a typical person even question, let alone reject their religion?

Senegal is around 95% Muslim, mostly aligned with Sufism, a form of mystical Islam that developed centuries ago. Sufis belong to brotherhoods, which have their own practices and are headed by *marabouts*. Everyone here tells me that Islam is the religion of peace, and it's true that Senegal is a great model for religious tolerance. Many families have both Christians and Muslims living side by side, and the Casamance separatist struggle was about the lack of developmental support from the northern government, not religious conflict.

Most Muslims, like most Christians, are not fundamentalist. The Senegalese are peaceful, loving and kind people – in fact, some of the most hospitable people I have ever met. But my feeling is that being peaceful, decent and kind is nothing to do with being Muslim or Christian. Rather, it's to do with being human. Most people are peaceful, loving and kind.

The fact that most Muslims do not engage in the activity practised by ISIS or Al Qaeda is surely not due to the teachings of their religion. It's because they use their humanity and commonsense to see beyond the ancient beliefs of the faith – or the fundamentalist perversions of them. It seems to me that religious organisations are man-made and political, with all the contradictions that come with that fact, while our relationship with the universe is something quite different, and certainly not something I could simplify to fit within any system of organised religious belief.

For Khady, none of this matters. She has her quiet faith in God, calls herself Muslim because her parents were, and that's about it. It's not surprising that it's the developing countries that tend to be most religious, as it seems to me the role of God in most people's lives is largely functional. Once the role of God as the provider can be easily met by the existence of plenty of jobs; as a protector by the presence of security from the State; and as a healer by the presence of a good health system, then his relevance declines, and only then can you tell who truly believes.

Senegal champions many great family and societal values that have fallen by the wayside in the Western quest for individuality and autonomy, but, as a Muslim society, it is a polygynous society, where multiple wives are common. And it's rare to meet a contented wife in such a household. There always seems to be jealousy. Most of the time, I think one of the reasons Khady wants to be with me – and indeed, other Senegalese women like to be with *toubab* guys – is that we're far less likely than an African man to take a second, or a third, or fourth wife. Well, that's that she thinks. I'm kidding of course. As my male Senegalese friends jokingly tell me, one problem is enough.

Sometimes Khady will wearily declare that she needs a second wife to help her. After all, that's how the tradition started, with multiple wives all helping each other in the family compound. I'm never totally sure whether she's joking or testing me to see if I'll go for it, but unless I converted to Islam it's a moot point.

Occasionally, I do wonder, though. After all, if humans, by nature mated for life and were very tightly bonded, then surely we wouldn't need all these marriage customs? Such proof of togetherness would not be deemed necessary – what to say of the question of multiple wives (or even husbands)?

Even though women here are primed from childhood

to know they'll be one of several wives, I've heard from a number of co-wives that nothing diminishes the broken-heartedness, the humiliation or the sense of betrayal they feel when the husband does take another. It is sad that these local traditions pit women against each other, reducing the likelihood that they will unite to fight for greater women's rights.

Where we *toubabs* are concerned, it seems it's not just the local men who indulge in polygamy. Pretty much every African in a relationship with a *toubab* has an additional local husband, wife, boyfriend or girlfriend – and often another (oblivious) *toubab*. Polygyny is in the DNA here, and normalised, even though doing it without the wives knowing about each other is neither normal nor allowed. Families seem to turn a blind eye, due to poverty and the hope for that trickle of European funds.

It's not at all unusual to hear of a European woman discovering that a local woman she had believed to be her husband's sister, or a maid, had actually been his other wife all along. What would be pretty much the worst possible life event in the West is so common here that it is deemed barely worthy of comment.

Perhaps one *toubab* friend of mine has it right, in that she is actively searching for a second, co-wife for her husband. She will never be able to provide him with children, and everyone knows all African men want kids, so why not accept the local customs instead of his cheating anyway? That shocked me in the early days, whereas now it seems like a perfectly rational decision, even if I do struggle with the sheer inequality of rights that allow a man to take several wives, while the reverse would never (officially) happen.

One French girl I knew met a youngish rasta guy in Abéné. She took the relationship seriously, broke off a long-term one in France and came back for three months to think about her future. Inevitably, I found out that the rasta had at least one other girlfriend and was also acting oddly, allegedly slipping local herbal medicines into her water to make her crazy for him. I couldn't stand by and watch, so I told her he had another woman, but I almost wish I hadn't.

He flagged me down as I drove along the high street one day and then dragged me out of the car, threatening to kill me. We shouted and screamed in front of a gathering crowd for a long time, but at no point did he show any guilt or admit he was in the wrong. I was seen as the bad guy.

The French girl scarpered and he, after professing he'd never love again, met and married another *toubab* a few weeks later, then moved to Europe. When he recently returned to Abéné to visit his pregnant African girlfriend, he acted as if we were best friends and nothing had happened. Memories do seem to be short.

I know of several Europeans married to locals who also have local spouses, but unless the *toubab* is a very close friend, I no longer say anything. This goes against my way of thinking, but I would rather be able to go on living here peacefully. Everyone hears these stories; every *toubab* knows what happens. Some turn a blind eye to the possibility and some truly believe their own story is different – as do I.

Many *toubabs* seemingly have little problem with converting to Islam in order to marry. A small number of them take this seriously, giving up alcohol, praying and believing, while others convert in name only, continuing to drink and eat bacon sandwiches – or at least they would, if bacon were available.

I often joke that Khady is really an animist, which she vehemently denies – before pouring *bounok* at the base of our *fromager* tree to appease its genie. She asked me if I would convert to Islam upon marriage. I told her that I am happy as I am, and need to remain true to myself. After some reflection, she declared that as long as I respect her belief, then that is fine. Perhaps realising which side their bread is buttered, her family agreed, and that's where we stand. The children will be another matter, but my intention is to let her explain her beliefs and I will explain mine, while also teaching them to think freely and to make up their own minds when they are old enough.

A key aspect of living with an African is that you never live with the African alone; there will always be an extended family to take into consideration, which is not without its challenges for a *toubab* used to individualistic ways. The African family, while a great thing, and a fantastic support system for the young and the old, has a tendency to hinder the development of individuals.

I heard the true story of a West African politician who eventually resigned, as he just couldn't support the tens, if not hundreds, of "relatives" who latched on to him for support. I've met expatriate Africans returning from Europe for a holiday who admit they only do so rarely, as they just can't afford all the gifts expected of them by their families.

Despite several so-called friends advising her to suck me dry, Khady realises she can have a better life in the longer term if she doesn't act that way. There are so many stories of mixed couples where the *toubab* can no longer stand the family demands and leaves. Or the *toubab* refuses point blank to meet those demands, and the African partner can't stand the family pressure. Again; game over. Finding a compromise both parties can live with seems to me to be the sensible route.

In the West, the rights of the individual are seen as the most important thing. In Africa, an individual is seen in terms of his or her relation to others; as a brother, a father, a son, a Muslim or Christian, a Diola and so on. Perhaps this explains why birthdays are rarely even known, and certainly not celebrated. Each of these relationships carries cultural obligations and expectations which are more important than individual rights.

It was when I realised this that I started to understand the clash of cultures that happens when Westerners seek to impose their own values, and can't fathom the thinking that rejects them: the right of a child to go to school as opposed to helping in the fields, the right to be in a homosexual relationship rather than to marry and produce children. I think this emphasis on relationship and the collective helps to explain these differences. Then you can throw into the equation the belief that failure to maintain the traditions of your ancestors brings bad luck.

I have had to accustom myself to thinking of my family in a much wider way than just Khady and the boys. At one point, it also included Fakeba, as well as Yamas one and two, Jumbo and Myamoona, and I found I developed emotional bonds with them, too.

So I was upset when Yama number one disappeared. She took a few days off to go to a wedding, fell ill and ended up in hospital in Dakar. We never found out what was wrong and her family didn't seem to know either. We've heard that she's fine now and her father keeps insisting that she will come back, so we kept the position open, but a year has passed and we've still not seen her. That's how it rolls here in Africa sometimes.

I hope she does return, though. She was great with the kids and made the best guacamole in Abéné. After a few months of searching, we found another Yama (it's an abbreviation of Mariama). New Yama is a sweet and shy 16-year-old village girl, who always asks me the English words for things and tuts if I have a beer.

Jumbo, the girl we'd unofficially adopted, also moved on. Her father had placed her in our care hoping that Khady would be a good, strong influence on her. She was a typical teenager, wanting to party every night, hang out with boys and so on. Khady could just about control her, but she obviously figured I'd be a soft touch. The moment Khady went to her village for a few days, Jumbo proudly showed me some skin-whitening product she'd bought – which Khady had banned her from using.

These products, very popular with African women, often contain harmful bleaches, and we'd been trying to raise her to be proud of her natural beauty. I'd hate for her to end up looking like one of the ghastly Michael Jackson caricatures that I occasionally see in The Gambia, so Jumbo found out that I'm also capable of strict parenting. It's funny how life goes. I don't think I'd ever envisaged myself ending up discussing such issues with an African teenage girl.

It's not uncommon for an old man to take on a young girl as a bride here in Senegal. Possibly this is why there doesn't seem to be any moral judgement made on older European women who take a young Senegalese husband (although Khady tells me it's unheard of for a significantly older Senegalese woman to take a younger husband, so this must be a special dispensation for *toubabs*).

Before Yama number one, we had employed a 20-year-old girl called Oumey, who was already divorced, having run away from her African husband, a man old enough to be her grandfather. I was disturbed when I discovered this was also happening under my nose. Khady kept ignoring a number that called her phone multiple times. I asked why and she told me it was an old man who was chasing after Jumbo, who was 13 at the time.

Jumbo eventually ran out of chances. She kept disappearing and not coming back at night. We'd call a meeting with her family and she'd agree not to do it again. We were responsible for her and would get the blame if she wound up pregnant, so on the third strike, Khady sent her back to her father's care. She was rumoured to be pregnant a few months later, although I've since seen her, childless, so either that was village gossip, or she saw some back-street abortionist.

Myamoona, Khady's niece, also stayed with us for some months. Her father, Tierno, had provided zero support since abandoning Khady's sister with four very young kids. When Myamoona arrived at the Little Baobab, her scalp was encrusted with pus-filled scabs. We cleaned her up, taught her to brush her teeth, bought her clothes, sent her to school, taught her some English (she can now count to 40), took her to The Gambia for a holiday and gave her a decent life. She soon fattened up to a normal weight for her age and craved my attention, as she clearly lacked a father figure or any decent care whatsoever.

But after she had been with us for a few months, and I had grown to love her like a daughter, we got wind that Tierno was going to take me to the police unless I returned her to the mother (the mother had left her with us, desperate for help). The family insisted we comply with his wishes. No one seemed to care at all about the child's welfare; only that we should obey the father and avoid trouble. So Myamoona went, and I felt I'd lost a little piece of my soul.

There have been times, though, when the demands

of the extended family have put so much pressure on my relationship with Khady that I thought it wouldn't survive. One such occasion was the all-important naming ceremony party for Alfie.

We'd been doing a lot of work on the land, including the building of new roundhouses, so money was tight, but Khady was under huge family pressure to throw a big party, and as far as they're concerned I'm a *toubab*, so I must have money. Khady told me just to give what I had. I told her the amount I did have, and everyone seemed happy.

Then, two days before the party, a message came from the family village with a price breakdown, totalling about four times the amount I had told them. We're talking several hundred pounds here – not peanuts.

"Well, I don't have it so what can I do?"

"You need to find it."

"But I don't have it."

And so on.

No one believed me, and the truth is, as a *toubab*, I can always find the money somewhere, even if it's on a credit card. The fact was, I couldn't see the importance of a ceremony for a baby who would know nothing about it. I understood the ceremony was important for Khady's family, and was more than happy to mark the event as best we could, but I was damned if I was going to fork out for a DJ who would play ear-splitting Nigerian auto-tuned pop for three solid days.

It always astonishes me that during such ceremonies the old people will sit passively as these sound systems play at levels that make me wince – and I'm someone who really misses rock concerts from back home. On the other hand, I've noticed that young Senegalese are as likely to blast out religious chants as they are pop music. The cultural distinctions between generations that Western youth cultures have created do not exist here, or in much of Asia.

The naming ceremony party is really all about the family's status, and nothing to do with the child. Everyone has these parties, and they always find the money. According to Khady, this is what people hide money away for. There often won't be the cash to send older children to school or feed them nutritiously, and people invariably wait too long before going to a doctor, and sometimes die as a result. But they will always have that party.

On this occasion, I felt justified in refusing. I wasn't just being stubborn, as I didn't have the money, and I'd been up-front about what I did have. But Khady said some nasty things to me, leaving me feeling that she and I were over, and that she was only staying with me because of the children.

When I discussed this with Fitty he laughed. "No Simon, this is how Senegalese women are. All women. She doesn't mean it, she's just angry. You must be strong." It seemed it was just another example of my not understanding.

After I'd spent the best part of a day feeling angry and seriously considering whether I stay or go, Khady came back in the evening as if nothing had happened. When I mentioned what she had said to me, she denied it, saying she'd been angry, but not with me; with her family. I had thought English women were complicated, but this was a whole new level.

Our cultural differences have created other tensions between us, too. There was the matter of Khady's mysterious chest pains and headaches, which were continuing unresolved despite various trips to different doctors.

One morning, I was sitting by Khady, cutting Alfie's hair as he fed. As we chatted, she seemed completely fine, then in a matter of seconds, her head slumped, she began to groan, her eyes rolled back and she started wailing.

"Help me, help me," she moaned, over and over, seemingly in agony.

She looked exhausted and dizzy.

"I'm going now," she muttered weakly, gently squeezing my hand. "Look after Gulliver, look after Alfie."

Death seemed imminent. Fighting nausea, I panicked and called Omar. "Call a car for the hospital."

"No, no," said Khady. "I no go hospital; this is mystic Africa."

Omar was in agreement. Western medicine had offered all it could. Now a *marabout* was required.

It was as if Khady had lost all control of her muscles, and she flopped listlessly. Before I knew it, neighbours and others started arriving, as if preparing for the worst. Further jets of fear passed through me and I fought back tears. They could wait.

I'd seen something like this before. People entering compounds where a *gris-gris* has been placed against them, and although seemingly healthy, suddenly losing all control and collapsing, or growing weak, as if cursed.

My feeling had always been that it's a mixture of perhaps a real medical complaint and psychology. This belief in mystic Africa, like the placebo effect, is strong. An electrician who worked on our house died following a dispute over a cow, after which someone had placed a curse on him. A few weeks later, he started bloating in size and then passed away.

Khady had talked of *jalangs*. A *jalang* is far more powerful than a *gris-gris* and can cause death. We have one to protect our house. I felt sad, scared, frustrated and weary. A stranger in a very strange land.

A car arrived. Khady had stabilised, so we gathered some things and set off for Bignona, where she wished to meet her uncle. Although she was still against the idea, I knew there was a hospital there as well. The car picked up another woman and we'd only driven a kilometre or two before Khady started chatting to her. By now, she had straightened up, and was laughing and joking as if there was nothing wrong.

"What's going on? You said you were dying a few minutes ago."

"I'm okay now. It must be our house, our land. It must be cursed by someone. I'm only ever ill there, not outside."

"But what about all the *gris-gris*, the goats' horns we've buried, the blessings from *marabouts*, the goat and chickens slaughtered...surely we're well protected? I told you it's all bullshit."

"There's something I forgot. In Ziguinchor, maybe five years ago, before we met, I went to a *marabout*. I was supposed to pay something later, but forgot. This is my punishment and why I'm suffering," she whispered.

My frustration increased. Why this now? Was she just thinking of any old reason? There was talk of the need to kill a cow, at which point I felt angry. Who'd have to buy the cow? Me, of course. I might think it's nonsense, but Khady believed it, and the illness would continue, and she might well die unless we took action. That was the reality of the situation, and I felt both scared and hijacked.

Of course much of the *marabout* talk is nonsense. Many traditional healers in Guinea died recently, having been convinced they could cure patients of Ebola. Thousands of dollars were put aside to educate those who survived, but a corrupt bureaucrat pocketed the lot.

Although Diola culture and traditions fascinate me and have been a rich inspiration, I felt unfairly pushed into the role of a passive observer. Perhaps this was the price I had to pay. I was exasperated, and let Khady make her own way to Bignona. I thought it best for her to sort this out alone. It was making me angry and confused.

When she returned, she told me she had been to the hospital, and spent £100 on prescribed medicine for a throat problem, paid for from our monthly food allowance. The hospital had insisted that it was a genuine medical condition, and nothing to do with mystic Africa.

"You were right all along," she said.

I asked to see the prescription (which surely will have included paracetamol, ampicillin and vitamin C tablets – in a region dripping with orange trees), in order to try to understand the problem. But Khady couldn't find it, or the bag with the medicines.

"I must have left it in the bush taxi. It's okay, we can buy some more."

Hmmm.

Relationships are hard enough when you have similar backgrounds. Believe me, I've tried. Throw in a completely different culture, education, religion and language barriers, and only the strong will survive. We're not talking English-French or English-Italian here; it's a whole new ball game, a clash of continents where we can each be completely and utterly bewildered by how the other reacts, or doesn't react. Never easy but rarely boring.

There have been occasions where it has all become too much and I can't believe I'm still here. It's no doubt the same for Khady, though. I'm sure I'm not so easy to live with.

One thing I've discovered – and other Europeans with Diola wives confirm the same – is that a Diola woman never backs down. Often I'm in the wrong if we've had an argument, but not always. If I don't make the first move towards reconciliation, however, I'm absolutely sure Khady would walk away.

"I managed before you and I'll manage without you," she'll declare. I have to say I admire her strength and dignity.

I've always felt that most of the *toubabs* here in Africa are mad, mercenary or missionary. I'm probably a bit of each. There are plenty who are escaping from something back wherever home is, and I'm determined not to end up like many, drinking myself into oblivion.

I have a beautiful wife and a beautiful family. I live in paradise and my work isn't really work; it's my passion, and I am living the dream. That has all been quite true for the most part, and it's very much the image I present to the outside world, but there have been many occasions when despite all of this, I have felt down.

Of course, no one has known, bar Khady. I'm good at bottling up my emotions. When my last marriage broke down I didn't tell a soul for more than ten months: a combination of pride, embarrassment and a stupid fear of disappointing others around me, although, in fact, they would have wanted to help. I knew my family would be upset, and I couldn't bear to tell them, even at the expense of my own wellbeing.

And yet, a few years later, I have found myself doing the same thing. On the outside, I have been communicating this perfect picture image through my website, and it's true that great things have been happening. But there have been incredible lows that even Gulliver's smile couldn't lift me out of.

Some of the issues I'd made out to be minor irritations were in actual fact massive issues that have confronted me every day, and often made me angry: the lack of privacy, knowing that Khady's primary responsibility would always be to her family rather than to me, the demands for money, the villagers' view of me.

When Khady and I are happy, everything is great, but on occasion, everything I do has seemed to annoy her. She has had her issues with me. Why couldn't I get her culture? Why was I annoyed to find some random local guy sitting in my house before I'd even risen in the morning? Why had I entered into a business arrangement with my mechanic when I could have used the money to help her?

I have asked myself, did I rush into this new life? Gulliver was hardly planned but I gladly took on my responsibility. Things always turn out best for people who make the best of the way things turn out, and I think one of my strengths has been to take the bull by the horns and tackle new challenges, despite past disappointments.

Nonetheless, one day all these feelings built to a crescendo. Khady and the kids were out and I found myself sitting, rocking back and forth on the side of the well, staring down into the murky depths below.

I was thinking back to my break-up with my first wife, Mikaela, and the cold dark winter nights of 2007. I would return from my stressful job to a cold, empty house and often not bother to eat. I'd just fill the bath and lie there until the water turned cold and I was shivering, sometimes just rolling out onto the floor and lying under a towel, waking in the early hours, then sitting drinking coffee till dawn, unable to comprehend what had happened. Night after night this happened, until I was so lonely I went online and found a new Mikaela, desperately trying to recreate what I'd lost. And that, of course, could never happen.

Here I was again, with that feeling of just wanting to let go, but rather than counting the number of times I have fallen, I have always tried to count the number of times that I have been able to pick myself up again. Failure is the basis of success. It helps me to understand my inner self, and that in turn allows me to overcome these failures. If I have one quality, then it is resilience.

Sometimes it has felt as if Khady and I would never understand each other, but then, as I thought deeper about our relationship, I started to realise that, despite the often vast differences, it was far more robust than the others I'd been in.

As one small example, I'd never before had an argument with my exes. I never felt the inclination. Mikaela always said I was so relaxed I was almost horizontal, and it frustrated the hell out of her. Khady and I, in contrast, were having the occasional screaming match. I'd storm off, then come grovelling back. After all she's a Diola and will never back down.

It was now clear to me that this was a good thing. We'd clear the air and then be happy again. Some of the cultural issues were recurring but as time went by we found solutions. Our new jungle bar area was working, and non-family and non-guests stayed there more now, giving me the privacy I'd lacked for so long. The fact that I had invested in Khady and helped her with businesses meant she was slowly becoming self-sufficient, and not having to make constant demands, which was important for the sanity of us both. We were growing a genuine partnership, enabling each other to reach our potentials in a way neither of us could alone.

As I continued to sit on the edge of the well and the sun began to sink, I started to feel more positive. Then I heard the squawking of birds. I looked up to see hundreds flying overhead, and within that mass of many species, I was sure that I could see a flash of red. I'm convinced it was a hornbill.

I returned to the house, still melancholy and scared for the uphill journey required to make this new life work, but feeling sure once more that I was on the right path.

Later, when Khady returned, Bob Marley played on her phone:

*Baby don't worry,*
*About a thing,*
*'Cos every little thing,*
*Gonna be alright.*

I joined in, embellishing somewhat:

"Woke up this morning,
Smiled at the rising sun,
Chased two hornbills
From my doorstep…"

# AFRICAN DELIGHT

*I hear the sound of drums across my land and I walk about, greeting people and stopping to watch Khady, who leads a chant in Diola – a call and response song honouring me and our sons.*

*I think about those that have moved on, of Fakeba, Yama, Myamoona and Jumbo, and hope they find their own happiness.*

*The people from Abéné that I care about are all here.*

*Jack (the) Wijnker is dancing up a storm on the dance floor – solo, naturally.*

*Eddie, my Irish friend, is around somewhere, but has disappeared to buy more bounok.*

*Khady's sister, Fatou, is dancing like a loon, all elbows and knees, whirling like a dervish.*

*Fitty and Skippy are drumming up a storm in the open area outside our house beneath a sacred fromager tree and beside the jalang.*

*Lamin the mechanic disturbs me, telling me I need a new clutch rubber. "Tomorrow," I say, "I'm busy."*

*Omar the driver is eyeing up one of my toubab guests.*

*Deanne is radiant in her white robes and flowing locks; an African queen.*

*Papis asks if we can play some Springsteen later.*

*Binta sways sensually, trying to make eye contact before giving up and moving on to someone else.*

There is an essay by Binyavanga Wainaina entitled "How to write about Africa," which lists many of the clichés that writers tend to make about the "dark continent". Huge, orange shimmering suns, smiling and vibrantly dressed dancing tribal people, the primal sounds of the drums, the wide-eyed snake-fearing boy...you get the picture.

There's a reason writers invoke these clichés but I guess it's only really an issue if they focus on them at the expense of the reality of modern Africa. I mention this because all of these clichés were present and correct at the party we were holding to celebrate Alfie, and this is my attempt at telling you about it without being clichéd.

Khady had reached a compromise with the family and everyone was happy again; hence the party. My friend Saly of Wakily was playing drums, along with Cherif Big Man, Fitty Futta and Skippy, who occasionally let his scowl relax and smiled warmly at me. Almost everyone knows the rhythms and how to drum here, but if they don't, they'll surely have a dance routine to put Michael Jackson to shame.

A gasp ran through the crowd as Soulyman the *mamapara* appeared, leaping and bounding, then stooping low and balancing on one stilt like the acrobat that he is. As he stood still, legs apart, a small figure went running towards him, passed between his stilted legs and held out his arms to be swept up for a bird's-eye view. Alfie still knows no fear.

Despite the difficulties and hardships, and a distinct lack of hornbills to chase, rarely a day passes when I don't feel like the luckiest man alive. Many travel in search of something, finding only what they bring with them, but I have found so much. I love my home, I love my friends, and most of all, of course, I love my boys and Khady.

Slowly, slowly our life improves. One day we may even get dial-up quality internet, though that might be wishful thinking. Along with guests, I now receive volunteers, who have the opportunity to come and work alongside us, finish some of those projects I may never get around to, and possibly, in the future, to bring skills such as teaching, allowing us to home-school the kids alongside their local education.

The boys play outside all day, and have a freedom that is a gift. While the English education system may turn out efficient, high performers, at what cost, when they are trained to use their abilities only for personal success? The system worships performance, selection and competitiveness, but I hear very little of the underlying philosophies of educating children.

Others here have given their kids a well-rounded education that has allowed them to go on to European universities, and I see no reason why we can't, if that is what they desire. I, for one, am very curious as to whether they'll embrace their African or their English side, or, instead, find a middle way.

My other major worries, around healthcare, are fading, as

I find better health facilities nearby, and also meet Western doctors who are moving to the region. Although we have had no further near-death experiences, Khady's headaches and chest pains continued and I'd given up believing there was a solution. I'd taken her to a great hospital, where they'd scanned her, but found nothing. Finally Khady went to yet another *marabout*. I exclaimed in disbelief, but she was convinced this one would work.

She returned holding a small scrunched-up piece of paper, unwrapping it to show me.

"What happened?" I asked.

"The *marabout* gave me a head massage and then squeezed it like this." She held her head tightly between the palms of her hands and twisted her face into a painful expression.

"This came out. It's the evil stuff, the stuff that was causing me pain."

She showed me the paper, in which there was what looked like a small, gooey lump of brown stuff, like a soggy stock cube or lump of hashish.

Surely this was a trick, a sleight of hand? Show some evidence to patients and they believe they are cured. The psychological power of the placebo is well documented. Whatever the truth, the headaches and pain seem to have disappeared, once and for all.

Sometimes crazy things happen, but it also has to be said that I am extremely lucky, and wonderful things often happen to me too. Recently, while having our land measured officially by a topographer, I was called to one side to be given some news.

"Simon, there's been a mistake. The fence is in the wrong place."

My heart sank. We'd have to move the fence and lose a strip of land.

"No, no, you own more land. That strip of land is yours." He pointed to a strip of 13 metres in width by about 100 metres in length, containing further forest and fruit trees.

I couldn't believe it, and felt like I did the day, four years earlier when the land seller's brother had negotiated me down a full third of the price that I'd originally agreed to, whereas almost every other *toubab* gets scammed or ripped off on their land purchases.

Then I received a message from my bank manager in Brikama in The Gambia, who explained that I'd received a few thousand euros from someone in Switzerland. It turned out to be from a lovely former guest. A year earlier we'd discussed building a house for her, which would be available to other guests in her absence. Without even telling me, she'd sent through the cash.

Somehow things roll along, despite the downturn in tourist numbers due to European austerity, the visa and the Ebola scares in previous years. During the busiest time, the Abéné festival, we've hosted more than 25 guests over a ten-day period. It was heartening to see so many people coming together, having a great time and putting money into the region.

New Year's Eve was another party to remember. We all

gathered on the beach to witness frenetic Sabar Wolof drumming from Dakar, as the audience tried to out-freaky-dance each other. On New Year's Day, in what is becoming an annual tradition, our small tribe took a day trip to a beach at the edge of the mangroves. The water there is as still as a millpond, miles from the nearest people and, according to my criteria, one of the hidden wonders of the world. We spent a day exploring, relaxing, swimming and drinking *bounok*, while Khady and the girls fried fish and prepared a fresh salad.

Miguel, my Portuguese friend, arrived, and together we grabbed a cold Gazelle beer each and, escaping the party for a few minutes, went to check out my garden. After a few years of struggle, watching plants drowning in the rainy season, plants and vegetables being eaten or crops not growing in the dead sand, I'd taken on board some of Miguel's permaculture techniques, and wanted to show him the results.

Walking into his botanical garden in nearby Kafountine is like entering a cool, jungle-like garden of Eden. Everything grows in abundance on raised bed terraces, so I was astonished when he told me he'd only begun a year or so earlier.

"At that point it was just flat, grey and sandy. It looked like a cement lot," he said.

I had stared at a three-metre-tall papaya tree with 20 or

more large fruit hanging from it like a bunch of giant grapes, and he had told me it was six months old and grown from seed. Holy cow! At that point in time, I had papaya twice as old, yet to reach shoulder height, and still showing no sign of fruiting.

And now, here we were, looking at my own raised compost beds with a jungle-like mix of trees, fruit, vegetables, medicinal plants and flowers. After months of backbreaking labour, involving copious amounts of blood, sweat and tears, I now have my own emerging green paradise, and yes, plenty of papaya.

I returned to the party, where I couldn't help but slink along to the rhythm of the drum. Despite being nearly blind, Khady's mother, Aida Mane, could still cook up a storm on the dance floor, and I joined her to bend forwards, stamp my feet and shake my out-stretched arms, much to the delight of the other Diolas. She was there along with Khady's brothers, Lamin and Mustafa. Mustafa was working himself up into a trance, and looked all set to bring out the knives.

Several years earlier I'd visited Alphouseynou and Aida Mane, presenting them with a bag of kola nuts – bitter seeds with a narcotic quality that are traditionally given during a marriage proposal. Khady's father had passed away shortly afterwards, so we'd had to wait, but now Aida reminded me not to forget.

As I reassured her, a familiar figure approached, and I was astonished to see that it was Khady's cousin, Insa, who had been missing from her village for our past few visits. He had a haunted look in his eyes, and explained to me that he'd paid hundreds of euros, raised by his village, to a boatman who had left, with an overloaded boat, from the Casamance coast. Before they'd even passed The Gambia the boat had hit a storm and tipped over. All Insa remembers is waking up on the beach, the sole survivor.

Khady told me that her younger brother now wished to try his luck. I told her to tell him to speak to me first. Most tales I hear involve gun wounds, drownings, being blown up or imprisonment. The few people I've met who have tried and failed won't talk about it.

A couple of friends had arrived earlier, fresh from the UK winter. I had taken them into a small shop soon after their arrival to buy some water. I wasn't sure whether to be irritated or delighted when a couple of rasta guys that I hadn't seen before immediately nodded at Simon and Emily, declaring "You've just arrived, haven't you?"

Then they turned to me. "And you live here." It was a declaration, not a question.

"How do you know?"

"Well, your friends look clean, smart and very white, but you..."

Feeling that I belong here is a long, slow process. I may never truly assimilate, in the same way that expats in the UK will always seem like immigrants to homegrown Brits, but I'm trying.

More than at any time I can recall, it seems that the world isn't working. Differences are growing between the developed and the less-developed world, between the secular West and the Muslim world, between the haves and the have-nots.

We're in the era of globalisation, but despite all the talk of diversity, we are more than ever trapped within our own identities and differences. They say the world is a village, but it seems to me to be a village of villagers who barely know each other. Instead of confidently celebrating our riches, we seem to prefer fearful conflict.

There is a conflict of perception in the world. Perceptions might result from ignorance but they often have more to do with feelings, with emotions and convictions. And we lack confidence in ourselves, in others and in the future. Instead, we fill our hearts and minds with fear, with doubt, with distrust. Rather than celebrate our differences, we use them to define ourselves, distracting ourselves from our ignorance, our fears and our doubts.

As I see it, the only way forward is to be confident in who we are, to question, to constructively criticise and to embrace complexity. Issues are rarely black and white, and I usually find myself on the fence, which often seems the most rational place to be. We need to be modest and to understand that we all look at the world through our own viewpoints.

There's so much noise in the modern age, but in the end, the world is changed by the examples we set, not by the opinions we give. Everything – our ideas, our perceptions, our religions and our imaginations – is just our points of view.

Once we can realise and accept this, we don't have to doubt everything. Instead, we could be enthusiastic and curious about the limitless number of other points of view out there, all perceiving exactly the same world in their own ways. We will for sure find many similarities and shared values.

I've often thought that the hardest part of any journey is taking that first step out of the door, leaving the comfort of home, of certainties, habits, friends and family. If you can make that step and understand other viewpoints, which almost certainly won't be nearly as different as you thought, then maybe you can find happiness.

Khady had saved the biggest surprise until the end. As I stood swaying to the rhythms and laughing with my friends, I started to hear a familiar chant and the percussive clatter of metal upon metal. About 40 women walked up our driveway, singing and making their beautiful racket. They formed a semi-circle and then the men joined in, marching up and down with their own chant, in front of our house.

Out of the gloaming appeared a mystical creature, the *koumpo*, the green reed-covered dancer who is believed to be a forest spirit. Children screamed and ran in terror as the *koumpo*'s accomplices, *Essamaye* the devil and *N'gomala* the gorilla, turned up and performed their own dances.

And then something rather special happened, something that neither I nor Khady had ever seen or heard of before.

As dusk fell, we were called into the circle with Gulliver

and Alfie. The *koumpo* made strange ethereal noises and had some communication with the group leader, who relayed the message, in Diola language, to the crowd. It was only afterwards that Khady explained to me what was going on.

We all had to sit huddled together while the *koumpo* moved towards us and then enclosed us within his reeds. Even given this close proximity, I had no sense of there being a person inside the *koumpo*, so maybe the Diola are right that it is a forest spirit.

Alfie lasted a couple of minutes before scampering off. He's a tough kid, though, and wasn't too fazed, unlike Gully, who was petrified. I continued to sit, legs spread out in front of me, and, thankfully, looking straight ahead, when the stake of the head of the *koumpo* came plunging down, over my shoulder, narrowly missing my head and slamming down into the sandy earth between my legs with a thud, way too close for comfort.

The *koumpo* spoke some more in its otherworldly voice, while Khady, myself and seemingly the entire audience held its breath. The leader of the dance troupe talked back to the spirit, and thus the conversation continued. As is the norm for me here, I sat, totally and utterly baffled as to what was going on.

It was only afterwards that Khady explained that essentially we were being protected. If we have any problems in life, the *koumpo* will be watching over us. I'll try to remember that next time I'm stopped at a police checkpoint.

Some of the reeds were plucked from the creature and

presented to Khady. The next day, she took them to the *gris-gris* maker who sewed them into leather pouches, and we all now wear one around our waist. We are protected and things are looking up.

"Now Simon, it's been three years since my father died. It's time to get married," declared Khady, looking very content.

Just as soon as I spy a hornbill to chase, I might just take her up on that.

# ABARAKA

Years of slow-build word of mouth via my blog, writing and general promotion on the internet have begun to pay off, to the point that we are rarely alone as a family, and I spend my evenings at the bar or around the fire telling my stories. I am always busy taking guests on boat trips, where we are often surrounded by schools of dolphins, on treks through the local mystical islands, on guided walks with professional Gambian bird spotters and on bush drives through the forests to the north, Kermit permitting.

Many guests return for multiple visits, among them Daddy Cool, who took up residence for a couple of months and will return next year, Becky who's becoming a regular Christmas visitor, Niels "Gonna-Gonna" the crazy Dane, Shaun "Daddy England", who's now building his own house here, Steve who rode all the way from Dublin on his motorbike, and Mart who's always up for an adventure.

There are many others, who have now become friends – some mentioned in this book – and I thank you all. One adventurous young couple even cycled here from Scotland.

Get in touch if you want to visit. Please bring cheese.

Big thanks to Dan and Andrew at Eye Books for believing in me enough to do this again, and to Clio for shaping up the words. And once again to Bert Stiekma for the cover image that, to me, perfectly sums up the contents.

Jeremy, my brother, renamed "Monkey" by Gulliver, and his family, visited and fell in love with the Little Baobab, Khady and the boys. Watching Karen, my sister-in-law, "diola flapping" is an image I won't forget in a hurry, and it was heartwarming to see Edie acting as the older "sister."

My parents also returned for their third visit. Each time is better than the last, as comfort levels steadily improve and we have slowly decorated, tiled, installed lights and running water. They could tell I was fitting in over here when, on arrival, the Gambian customs official cried out my name and hugged me. And once he realised they were my parents, he hugged them too.

*Squirting Milk at Chameleons*, my first book, very much like my first son, popped out relatively easily. My second son Alfie took hours of torturous pushing and nearly finished Khady off. While not wishing to compare the writing of a book with the agony of childbirth (even though that is exactly what I am doing), this tome certainly feels like my Alfie. Losing the use of about ten letters of my laptop keyboard didn't help. Technology doesn't last long with the dust and humidity but "cut and paste" was my friend.

Lastly, I probably understated in my first book exactly how my family had felt when I embarked on this adventure.

You know those conversations where you explain that not only are you going to go and live in Africa but that you've met a local tribal girl and that you'll build a mud house together?

Oh, and by the way, you're going to be grandparents…

That didn't go down so well, initially. Of course they wanted me to be happy, but also to see me now and again, and they were confused as to what I was doing with my life. As was I, to be fair.

Often I find it easier to communicate my idea on the page, and publication of my first book gave them something tangible to explain exactly what I was doing.

I was very pleased with it, but my father telling me how proud he was meant the world to me.

*Simon Fenton*, Abéné, Senegal, June 2016

Check out Simon's website to book your own visit to the Little Baobab, to view films and images, to subscribe to his blog or check out his first book, Squirting milk at chameleons.

**www.thelittlebaobab.com**

# THEIBOUDJENNE

Here's Khady's recipe for *theiboudjenne*. Invite your friends and share the *teranga*.

1. Heat a good splash of vegetable oil then add 4 or 5 desert spoons of tomato puree, a couple of chopped tomatoes, a finely chopped onion and a little salt and pepper.

2. Meanwhile, prepare the vegetables. They're cooked in huge chunks, each the size of a fist: carrot, aubergine, cassava and a cabbage (local cabbages are small and white). You could use other vegetables like potato or sweet potato if cassava is hard to come by. Khady often also includes a small bitter vegetable that is related to aubergine.

3. Add 3 large cups of water to the pan. Bring to the boil and add the vegetables plus another pinch of salt. Boil for 15 minutes, then add the fish (whole fish with heads removed and cut in half). Cook for a further 15 minutes at a simmer. Note: Senegalese vegetables are very tough (they grow in sand) and require more cooking. These times may need to be reduced slightly to avoid mushiness.

4. Grind one chopped onion, 3 or 4 garlic cloves, a stock cube, peppercorns and a healthy pinch of salt.

5. Remove the vegetables and fish from the liquid. Add the ground onion mixture and rice (1/2 mug per person) to the liquid in the pan. Cover and simmer for a further 20

minutes).

6. Fry off the fish to crisp up the skin in a separate pan.

7. In Senegal, we include a dollop of bissap per person. This is a local green leaf, whisked up (often with some okra and a pinch of stock cube) to form a frothy mousse. You could try experimenting with some cooked spinach and okra.

8. We also serve with tamarind pods, which have a sharp pickle-like taste. Khady puts the vegetables and fish on top of them when removed from the stock in stage 5. The resulting liquid forms a tangy jus to pour over the meal.

9. Serve the bed of rice on a large platter with vegetables and fish on top. All sit round and dig in.

# GLOSSARY

Exact spellings are often unclear; these are my interpretations.

**Abaraka:** the Arabic for thank you that is also standard in the Diola and Mandinka languages.

**Alhamdouilalah:** "I thank God", an Arabic phrase that is widely used in West Africa and often painted on the front of buses.

**Assalaamu alaykum:** "Peace be upon you". An Arabic greeting used across North and West Africa. The correct response is Alaykum assalaamu.

**Attaya:** very strong and very sweet tea.

**Balanta:** the most populous ethnicity of Guinea Bissau and common in the Casamance, originating from the Guinea highlands.

**Banku:** mud blocks used for building houses.

**Bantaba:** a hut or shelter used as a meeting place. Ours is a thatched-roofed shelter we'd originally built to use for shelter while building our first house.

**Baobab:** large, distinctive trees, which are a national symbol of Senegal.

**Bassari:** a traditional minority tribe that inhabits the mountains of south-eastern Senegal and across the border into the highlands of Guinea.

**Baye Fall:** disciples of a Sufi Islamic sect founded by Cheik Bamba, who protested against French colonialism.

**Bissap:** a green leaf that is puréed into a gloopy sauce, served with fish and rice. Also the name of the hibiscus plant that is used to make a sweet Ribena-like juice.

**Boily boily:** hot in the Diola language.

**Bolong:** a creek or river.

**Boubou:** a long kaftan-type robe worn by Muslim men and pronounced "boo boo".

**Bounok:** Diola for palm wine. It is the fermented sap of the palm tree. When freshly tapped it is a deliciously sweet fruit juice, only very mildly alcoholic. Over the course of a couple of days, the sugar turns to alcohol and you have to hold your nose while drinking.

**Branco:** Portuguese and Guinea Bissauan creole for white man.

**Bukut:** the Diola initiation ceremony.

**Bumster:** unemployed Gambian hustler, offering various "services" to tourists.

**Cadeau:** fermented juice of the cashew apple.

**Café touba:** spiced sweet coffee.

**Cana:** local rum.

**Casamance:** the southern region of Senegal, sandwiched between The Gambia and Guinea Bissau, along the banks of the river Casamance.

**CFA:** West African francs pronounced "Sayfer." A unit of currency used in much of Francophone Africa and Guinea Bissau, fixed to the euro at a rate of around 655 francs to one euro or 800 to the £.

**Dagga:** an informal drinking shack, usually serving local hooch out of the back of somebody's house.

**Dalasi:** the unit of currency in The Gambia. There are currently (in 2016) about 60 dalasi to the £.

**Diola:** the tribe and language centred around the Casamance, southern Gambia and parts of Western Guinea Bissau. It is pronounced "Jola" which is also how it is spelt in The Gambia.

**Djembe:** a drum common in West Africa and well known in the West.

**Essamaye:** sometimes abbreviated to Si or Si-Si. A devil-like masked dancer.

**Fataya:** small ravioli-like deep-fried meat- or fish-filled pasties. Girls will sell them in the late afternoon from baskets on their heads; one of the few savoury snacks available to buy in Abéné.

**Fromager:** large, buttressed tropical tree, sometimes known as Kapok. The wood is used by the French to make the boxes for cheese, e.g. Camembert, hence the name.

**Fula:** an ethnicity spread across the Sahel region from Senegal to Cameroon. They are notably lighter-skinned than other peoples of West Africa, and are believed to have migrated from the Nile valley.

**(The) Gambia:** this tiny country is officially prefixed by "the" as it is named after "the" river Gambia that originates in the Guinea highlands, crosses eastern Senegal and then runs the entire length of its namesake country. Legend has it that the British sailed upriver firing a cannon to both the north and south. Where the cannon balls landed was where the border was drawn. This is highly unlikely as, although for much of its length the country is only 20 kilometres in width, this is a lot further than cannons of that time period could fire.

**Gamou:** Islamic gathering involving a night of praying and chanting with a marabout.

**Gare Routière:** the bush taxi and bus station.

**Gazelle:** a popular brand of local beer. It's light, making it perfect for hot climates, and is my favourite.

**Geli-geli:** small minibus crammed full of people and luggage for cheap public transport. Known as toca-toca in Guinea Bissau

**Genie:** spirits that inhabit large trees. Pronounced "guinea."

**Gomala:** a gorilla-like masked dancer.

**Griot:** oral historians and praise singers of the ancient West African empires that tell the histories of families at ceremonies. They are known as Jeli in Mandinka. Griot is pronounced "gree oh."

**Gris-gris:** protective talisman worn around the body. Usually a piece of Arabic scroll wrapped and sewn up in leather. Also known as ju-ju or amulet. Pronounced "gree-gree."

**Harmattan:** winds that blow down from the Sahara in the early part of the year, bringing much dust.

**Insh'allah:** "God willing" and all-round useful phrase (will you give me money? Tomorrow, insh'allah).

**Jaifonday:** large African lady's bottom.

**Jumbo:** popular salty stock cube that makes everything taste the same.

**Kankurang:** mystical masked creature that accompanies boys during Mandinka initiation ceremonies, or terrorises villages as a form of social control, depending upon your view.

**Karité (beurre de karité):** Shea butter that is sold cheaply in its pure form and used as a cure-all, as well as for massaging babies and as a skin moisturiser, thus explaining the fantastic complexions of most Senegalese. It is great stuff, but it reeks and makes me gag when Khady sticks a lump up each nostril if I have what is known locally as a "fresh cold." Western pharmaceutical companies use only a small percentage, mixed with perfumes and oils, in expensive blends that are too weak to give real benefits. It is found in the nuts of a tree that grows in eastern Senegal.

**Karoninke:**  predominantly Christian Diola tribe, inhabiting the mangrove swamp islands to the south of Kafountine.

**Kembo:**  tough and termite-resistant wood used by the Diola to make fences.

**Kola:**  bitter nuts with traces of amphetamines as well as caffeine, originating in West Africa. Formerly a currency, and still presented as gifts during ceremonies. A certain popular drinks company used them in their original formula, along with coca leaves.

**Koriteh:**  local name for Eid-al Fitr, the feast marking the end of Ramadan.

**Koumpo:**  dancer covered in green reeds that becomes possessed by a spirit and spins out of control.

**Lutte:**  traditional wrestling that is popular in Senegal and The Gambia.

**Maffe:**  peanut-based sauce, known as domoda in The Gambia.

**Mandinka:**  ethnicity, tribe and language centred around The Gambia and parts of Casamance.

**Mamapara:**  masked stilt dancer from the Mandinka tribe. Known as chakaba in Wolof.

**Marabout:**  holy man, traditional healer and provider of gris-gris. Pronounced "maraboo".

**Mbalax:**  aggressive and percussive Senegalese pop music, using sabar and tama drums. Popularised internationally by Youssou N'Dour.

**Nyankotan:** basic rice dish.

**N'yass:** masked creature present at koumpo dances.

**Peul:** different name for the Fula tribe.

**Pirogue:** dug-out canoe or larger wooden fishing boat.

**Quincaillerie (French):** hardware store.

**Ramadan:** the holy month of Islam, commemorating when the Quran was revealed to Mohammed. Fasting takes place from dawn till dusk.

**Seorouba:** two-drum set, placed over the knee and played by Mandinka musicians.

**Sept Places:** Peugeot bush taxi that carries the driver and seven passengers.

**Tabaski:** also called Eid al-Kebir, commemorates Abraham's readiness to sacrifice his son on God's command and the last-minute substitution of a ram. Every Islamic family that has the means will purchase a ram, of which they eat one third, give one third to their friends and donate the final third to the poor.

**Talibe:** a disciple of an Islamic holy man. Talibe boys often beg for cash in bus stations.

**Tapalapa:** French-style baguettes made fresh every morning in every village.

**Teranga:** a Wolof word, meaning hospitality or welcoming generosity. The national Senegalese football team is known as the Lions of Teranga.

**Theiboudjenne:** Senegalese national dish consisting of fish, vegetables and rice cooked in stock. Known as benachin in The Gambia.

**Touba:** holy city in northern Senegal, which is the site of a yearly pilgrimage, the grand maghal, for the Baye Fall brotherhood.

**Toubab:**  a non-derogatory term for white man. Urban legend says it derives from boys asking colonials for "two bob" coins, although I doubt this is true.

**Wolof:**  the predominant ethnicity of Senegal, descended from the Jolof empire. The Wolof language is the most common African language across the entire country, and also widely spoken in The Gambia.

**Yassa:**  a popular sauce made from onions, lemon and mustard, and eaten with fish or chicken and rice.

**For further information**

Simon and the Little Baobab: **www.thelittlebaobab.com**

Overlanding West Africa: **www.overlandingwestafrica.com**

How to write about Africa: **http://granta.com/how-to-write-about-africa/**

Art Oasis, Miguel's botanical garden in Kafountine: **www.artoasis.es**

For more information about the powers of djembe drumming, check out: **www.dougmanuel.com**

# About Eye Books

Eye Books is a small independent publisher that passionately believes the more you put into life the more you get out of it.

It publishes stories that show ordinary people can and do achieve extraordinary things.

Its books celebrate "living" rather than merely existing.

It is committed to ethical publishing and tries to minimise its carbon footprint in the manufacturing and distribution of its books.

www.eye-books.com

eye books

About Extraordinary Things Done by Ordinary People

# About the Author

Simon Fenton is a travel writer and photographer. After an early career in the morgues and pools of southern England, he lived, worked and travelled in Asia for several years, travelling independently through bush, mountain, desert and jungle, financing himself by teaching English, acting in Bollywood movies and working as a pig farmer in Vietnam.

He returned to "settle down", got married and set up the award-winning social enterprise StreetShine before a perfect storm of events re-ignited his wanderlust.

He eventually found himself in Senegal, where he and his Senegalese partner Khady have built – and run – an eco guest house (information at www.thelittlebaobab.com). They have two sons, Gulliver and Alfie.

A first book chronicling Simon's adventures in Senegal, *Squirting Milk at Chameleons*, was published by Eye Books in 2015.

# Praise for *Squirting Milk at Chameleons*

A must-read for anyone wanting an inside knowledge of the culture and lifestyle in Senegal. An entertaining and illuminating read, and highly recommended.

*Harriet King*
*Deputy Ambassador, British Embassy, Dakar, Senegal*

This book comes the closest that I've read to an outsider understanding our culture.

*Kemo Conteh*
*Development and governance consultant, Banjul, The Gambia*

Simon shares his journey with us, he shares his courage, vulnerability, and his faith. His story is an example of what life is really about. This book is a great and easy read and is a must for anyone wanting to understand the mystical side of Africa through a Westerner's eyes. Highly recommended!

*Doug Manuel*
*Creator of 'Do You Speak Djembe?'*

Simon Fenton invites you to share a seat in his *sept-places* taxi as it bounces through the steamy forests of the Casamance, navigating the myriad pleasures – and potholes – of his unexpected new life in the south of Senegal. It's sure to get a bit hot, cramped, and sweaty, but it's the best ride you'll take all year!

*Sean Connolly*
*Author of the* Bradt guide to Senegal

Simon's observations on the trials and tribulations of everyday life in West Africa are so true to how things work in this little visited part of the world. His charming and often funny stories always remind me of first moving to Africa and his positive take on all that Senegal can throw at him is a joy to read. I am sure his beautifully crafted tales will inspire others to break away from the crowd and strive to live a life that is full of adventure.

*Lawrence Williams*
*Founder/manager of Makasutu, The Gambia*